God's
Answers to
Tough
Questions

*Everything You Wanted to Know
but Were Afraid to Ask*

Marie D. Jones
Randy Petersen
Consultant: Gary Burge, Ph.D.

 Publications International, Ltd.

Marie D. Jones is an ordained minister and a contributing author to numerous books, including *Sisters, Mother, Grandmother, Friends, Graduation, Wedding,* and *A Mother's Daily Prayer Book.*

Randy Petersen is the author of *The Path to Heaven, The Powerful Prayer of Jabez,* and *Why Me, God?* He has also contributed to more than 20 other books, such as *The Revell Bible Dictionary* and *The Christian Book of Lists,* and to a wide variety of magazines, including *Christian History.*

Gary Burge is a professor in the department of Biblical and Theological Studies at Wheaton College. He holds a Ph.D. in New Testament from King's College, The University of Aberdeen in Aberdeen, Scotland. He is a member of the Biblical Archaeological Society and the Institute for Biblical Research.

Unless otherwise noted, all Scripture quotations are taken from the *New Revised Standard Version* of the Bible. Copyright © 1989 by the Division of Christian Education of the National Council of the Churches of Christ in the USA. Used by permission. All rights reserved.

Scripture quotations marked NIV are taken from *The Holy Bible, New International Version.* Copyright © 1973, 1978, 1984, International Bible Society. Used by permission of Zondervan Publishing House. All rights reserved.

Manufactured in U.S.A.

8 7 6 5 4 3 2 1

ISBN: 1-4127-1026-X

Contents

There Are No Dumb Questions

"This might be a dumb question, but—"

"Stop right there," the teacher interrupted.

The timid student halted in mid-sentence, mouth still open, bracing for a criticism of some kind.

"There's no such thing as a dumb question," the teacher said. "If you don't know something, the *smartest* thing you can do is to ask a question. Don't ever call it dumb!"

Unfortunately, both Christians and non-Christians have been shy about asking basic religious questions. What is God like? What did Jesus do? Why should I believe the Bible? These questions aren't "dumb"—they're important matters of faith and life. What was that tabloid tagline? "Inquiring minds want to know"? Well, if people have inquiring minds about celebrity gossip, how much better is it to inquire about truly important things concerning God, heaven, and the end of the world?

Some of these questions have clear answers from the Bible, which we'll offer you. Other answers are matters of opinion, or there might be different interpretations. We have tried to present the major views when no single view is acceptable to all. In any case, the following answers are those that have been voiced by the leading Christian thinkers of our generation.

We hope our answers will bring some clarity to the commonly asked questions regarding God, as well as inspire you to study the Scriptures for yourself.

CHAPTER ONE

Understanding God and Our World

*P*eople have always been fascinated with time. It is not surprising, therefore, that they would wonder how everything got started. In fact, people still debate that issue. Some argue that a big bang occurred and that the universe has been expanding ever since. Others think that the universe flows in an eternal cycle with no beginning and no end. Jews and Christians, however, believe God created all things and has always existed.

Q: If God created the world, who created God?

A: God has always existed as the eternal, personal deity from whom all life has manifested. There has never been a time when God did not exist, nor will there ever be a time when God does not exist. "I am the Alpha and the Omega," says the Lord God, "who is and who was and who is to come" (Revelation 1:8).

Nothing created God, for God is the only Creator. When Moses asked God to identify himself, God said, "I Am who I Am" (Exodus 3:14). In other words, God has no limits; he is without a beginning or an end. Indeed, he is the very one who gives all of creation its beginning and end.

Q: Why did God decide to create the world?

A: Imagine a painter who longs to create a great work of art but has no paints and no canvas upon which to create his or her masterpiece. By giving himself an outlet for his creative energy and using the universe as a canvas upon which to work, God opened the way for his love to be expressed, his compassion to be made real, and his joy to be made visible. We might say that the whole of creation is God's canvas. Each living thing, every bird of the sky or creature of earth or sea, is a part of the tapestry of creation that the Master Artist has brought into being.

God desired to express himself, and therefore he created the world as his means of expression. God first created light and darkness, and the division of day and night, and then created the heavens and the earth, and all the living things, finally creating his greatest work—humankind.

The act of creation brings God delight and even more joy to his relationships with those who love him. We are his masterpieces. Each of us is an individualized expression of God's glorious work, and it is because of our devotion to him that God created the world in the first place.

Q: The Bible says that, after God created the world, "it was good." Sometimes when I look at the world, it seems to be anything but "good." Why?

A: When God first created the world, it was, indeed, "good." In fact, it was heaven on earth. There was no evil, sin, war, crime, greed, poverty, or destruction of the environment. These things that we see as "not good" came about after Creation when people started to disobey God. We can see the terrible effects that have resulted from human sins, and we should be reminded that none of this was

God's will. God's will and intent was, and is, always good, pure, and positive.

God creates only good, but people decided to rebel against God. Many of the evil and tragic things you see are the consequence of people behaving contrary to God's laws, which he has given us from the beginning. Meanwhile, God uses suffering to draw us to him or make our characters and our faith stronger.

Q: Did God create Satan? Or is the devil some sort of rival to God?

A: God created all things, and that includes Lucifer, the Fallen Angel, who became known as "The Tempter" or "Satan" (Matthew 4:1–3; Luke 10:18). Lucifer thought himself more beautiful than all other angels, and his vanity and narcissism caused his fall from grace and his rebellion against God. He chose to oppose God and all God stands for, and thus he became the devil. God did not make him evil; he chose this path for himself.

Because God is all-powerful, and Satan is not equal in power to God, Satan is not a rival force.

Nevertheless, he does have some power and can influence people to an extent, especially in the areas of temptation, sin, and desire. Satan tempted Adam and Eve, and they disobeyed God. He has tempted people from the beginning, and people have often succumbed. Jesus, however, was one who always stayed true to God's will. In the wilderness, for example, Jesus refused to give in to both physical and spiritual temptations, thus showing us that we, too, can resist Satan's wiles (Luke 4:1–13).

Q: Why did God create the Garden of Eden in the beginning?

A: God wanted people to live in paradise, and so he created the Garden of Eden where all life co-existed in perfect harmony and where he placed Adam and Eve, the first man and woman. The Garden of Eden was a lush and vibrant garden in the East near the land of Havilah at the junction of the Tigris and Euphrates rivers. This garden represented the perfection of the natural world, filled with all good things that were pleasing to the eye and to the palate of human beings.

God placed Adam and Eve into this blessedly
abundant garden to be responsible stewards of
God's creation. It was here, in this garden of
absolute plenty, that all of the birds and fish and
beasts were brought before Adam so that he could
give them names. It was also here that the serpent
(Satan) tempted Eve with the promise of gaining
wisdom by eating a fruit from the one tree God
commanded them not to touch—the Tree of the
Knowledge of Good and Evil.

Q: Why were Adam and Eve cast out of
paradise?

A: Adam and Eve were sent out of the Garden of
Eden because they disobeyed their Creator, who had
forbid them from partaking of the fruit of the Tree
of the Knowledge of Good and Evil. They not only
introduced sin into the world but they also were no
longer worthy to remain in paradise.

People have often held Eve responsible for the Fall
of humankind. After all, she initially gave in to the
temptation of the serpent, who had promised that

she would become Godlike and never die if she ate from the tree. Eve saw that the tree was beautiful and its fruit ripe and lush, so she ate the fruit. Adam, however, is also to blame. God had specifically told him not to eat this fruit, and he still did anyway.

Interestingly, Adam blamed Eve, and Eve blamed the serpent for their transgressions. Indirectly, they blamed God himself, for God had given Eve to Adam and God had allowed the serpent into the garden. Despite their refusal to confess their sins, God was merciful to them. He cast them out of the garden, thus barring them access to the Tree of Life so they would not be eternally bound to their sins. More importantly, he gave them and humankind hope by promising that the devil would ultimately be defeated and a Savior would come to redeem those who are faithful to him.

Q: Did God make Adam and Eve to be equal? Or was Eve less than Adam?

A: The account in Genesis of God's creation of Adam and Eve says, "So God created humankind in his image, in the image of God he created them; male and female he created them" (Genesis 1:27). Although God had made a distinction between humans and other living beings when he said humans would have dominion over animals, he did not rank the man and the woman. They were both blessed with his likeness, so how could one be superior over the other? It would be like saying one part of God is superior to another part.

Moreover, Genesis also notes, regarding the union between a husband and wife, "Therefore a man leaves his father and his mother and clings to his wife, and they become one flesh" (2:24). If they are one, how can value distinguish them? God gave them the same responsibilities, the same laws, and the same ability to enjoy his physical and spiritual blessings; accordingly, he made them equals.

Q: God made humanity as male and female. But are women equal to men?

A: In the eyes of God, man and woman are equals. God gave men certain gifts and abilities, and he gave women certain gifts and abilities. These gifts do not make either men or women superior. And most importantly, he created men and women to be partners with each other.

Jesus counted women among his most loyal and devoted followers. He loved and respected women, and he never turned away from them. His mother, Mary, has become the most revered woman of all time, and no Christian would ever argue that she was lesser in the eyes of God than any man. It was women who supplied the needs to his band of followers; it was women who were nearest to him when he died on the cross; and it was women to whom he first appeared after his resurrection from the dead. This may not imply that Jesus regarded women more highly than men, but it certainly shows that he did not regard them any less.

God created all humanity in his image. His essence is present in both genders. We will come to a place in our lives when we will know the Kingdom of Heaven on earth and understand what Jesus meant when he said, "For whoever does the will of my Father in heaven is my brother and sister and mother" (Matthew 12:50).

Q: Does God want to rescue his people from this world, or does he want to save this world?

A: The Bible tells many stories of God rescuing people from the dangers of this world—whether these dangers be from people or nature. Often, God appears just in time to perform a miracle. In the New Testament, God performed his greatest miracle when he sent his only Son, Jesus Christ, to rescue us from our sins.

Yes, God does want to rescue us. He even desires to save the world, but much of the world has either ignored him or engaged in terrible deeds to show their hatred of him. Because evil has corrupted this world so much, God has promised "a new heaven and a new earth" where "he will wipe every tear from [our] eyes. Death will be no more; mourning and crying and pain will be no more" (Revelation 21:1, 4).

Meanwhile, God does not rescue us by taking us out of this world or by secluding us in some protected area away from the rest of the world. What would happen if God saved us from every terrible thing? If God always rescued us, we would never learn to be strong, courageous, and compassionate in our faith. And we would never have the opportunity to show that compassion to a needy world.

Q: Since God instructs his people to be good stewards of what he has given them, should Christians be committed environmentalists?

A: We have been made stewards and guardians of the abundant world God has placed us upon, and yes, we as Christians must commit to protecting and nurturing the earth and all her glorious creatures. To not do so would be an insult to God and to his desire for us to live in abundance and diversity. God gave us *dominion* over the earth. He did not give us *domination*. We have been entrusted with a serious task, and we must take it seriously, or we risk offending God.

By caring for the land, the water, and the air, we not only become good stewards of our world but also of the world our children and their children will inherit. We would be sinful if we left the future generations a devastated environment because of our own selfish greed and ignorance. God created the world for us to enjoy and experience in all its fullness, and to be wasteful and irresponsible lets God know that we are unappreciative and undeserving of his love and good graces.

Anything we can do to make the earth cleaner, safer, and healthier not only benefits our children and us but also is a way of saying "thank you" to the loving God who provided us with such a beautiful planet to call home.

⌘

Q: Did God create other "worlds" in addition to our world somewhere in the universe?

A: The Bible tells us that God created the entire universe, including everything within it, as well as what may lie beyond it. As modern science progresses and as we acquire the ability to see farther and farther into the depths of the cosmos, we may discover many other worlds just like ours, all crafted by the masterful hand of God, the ultimate artist and creator of worlds.

Though the Bible focuses mainly on this world and the lives of men and women here on earth, we do know that there are heavenly places, and hellish ones, too, and that God is the all-powerful Creator and overlord of all those otherworldly places. Imagine how interesting and fascinating it would be to one day meet beings from other planets and discover their own perceptions of God. Would they imagine God to be the same way we do? Would they call God "God" or something we cannot understand or pronounce? Would they know the Bible? That is all speculation, of course, but the Bible does not discount the possibility.

Science has already proven that the universe is far more vast and amazing and filled with more planets, suns, and solar systems than we ever imagined. But even science cannot explain what created that first spark of life that gave birth to all we know. That lies in the realm of religion, which proves to us through our steadfast faith that God is the intelligent force behind all creation, whether it be the trees in our own backyard or the galaxies ten billion light years from earth.

CHAPTER TWO

God's View on Suffering and Evil

*W*hen we see the massive devastation of an
earthquake on a newscast, we can't help but
wonder why there had to be so much human suffering.
When we read the horrifying account of a child predator,
we can't help but question why this evil person was not
extinguished long ago. It is even more puzzling and
disturbing when we see a loved one enduring terrible pain
or when we personally witness the casualties of evil. God is
all-powerful and all-good, and there are reasons why he
allows suffering and evil to be present in our world.

Q: How can God understand my suffering?

A: Because God is all-knowing, he not only knows
our every thought, desire, and intention but also
understands our suffering. He knows our hearts and
our innermost fears. He knows our souls and our
spirits. In fact, he knows our prayers even before we
pray them. His wisdom is infinite, and that's why he

knows our innermost sorrows and pains and grieves for us.

Our heavenly Father created us to feel joy and to live life abundantly, but when we succumb to evil temptations or selfish desires, the consequences of such actions or thoughts invariably bring suffering. Some sins may be pleasurable for a time, but eventually we will suffer for our misdeeds.

Despite our disobedience, God is always ready to welcome us into his arms and grace. Nevertheless, it is up to us to repent of our sins and reclaim our divine heritage. It does not mean that our suffering will instantly vanish, but at least we have God's strength to endure any hardships or afflictions.

Just because God is the Creator of the universe does not mean that he cannot relate to the daily events of our human lives. In fact, he probably understands us better than we understand ourselves, especially since his Son took on the form of a human being. "For we do not have a high priest [Jesus] who is unable to sympathize with our weakness," wrote the author of Hebrews, "but we have one who in every respect has been tested as we are" (Hebrews 4:15).

No one has suffered physically and emotionally more than Jesus. His closest friends abandoned him when he was arrested; he was scourged and beaten; nails were driven into his hands and feet; people taunted him while he hung on the cross; and, moreover, his heavenly Father withdrew from him when he bore the sins of the world while he died on Golgotha. We can never understand to what depth Jesus suffered for us, but we can be certain that he understands our every suffering.

Q: Isn't it odd that Jesus was the Son of God and yet he suffered? What does this mean?

A: Jesus was not just the Son of God, but he was also the Son of Man (see Luke 19:10). Not only was it important for Jesus to become a human being so God could fully understand our sufferings, but it was also important so we could know to what length God would go to save us from our sins. Such knowledge assures us of God's deep love for us.

Moreover, Jesus came to earth to live as an example for all of us. By his perfect example, we know how we can best please our heavenly Father, how we can live life to the fullest, and how no amount of suffering can rob us of the joys in being a beloved child of God.

The resurrection of Jesus from the dead also gives us great hope. "In the world you face persecution," Jesus told his followers. "But take courage, I have conquered the world!" (John 16:33) Despite all that Jesus suffered, he still defeated death. That tells us that no suffering is too great for Jesus, and that's why he beckons us with the words: "Come to me, all you that are weary and are carrying heavy burdens, and I will give you rest. Take my yoke upon you, and learn from me; for I am gentle and humble in heart, and you will find rest for your souls. For my yoke is easy, and my burden is light" (Matthew 11:28–30).

As the Son of God, Jesus clearly showed us how to reconnect with God. As the Son of Man, Jesus showed us the way to walk in faith and live in grace, despite the suffering we experience. He took on our sufferings as his own, and he died for our sins so that we, too, could have eternal life with our Father in heaven.

Q: Does God suffer?

A: Jesus is God, and he certainly suffered. But does God the Father suffer? In the Parable of the Prodigal Son, it is evident from Jesus' perspective that God does suffer (see Luke 15:11–32). Like the father in the story, our heavenly Father is not just concerned for the physical and emotional welfare of his children but yearns for them to return to him. Knowing that his son has thrown his life away deeply hurt the father in Jesus' story. In effect, Jesus is telling us how God feels about us when we abandon him or give in to a sin; he anguishes over broken relationships.

As much as it grieves God when people reject him or when his own children disobey him, he is even more saddened to see his children suffer for their faith in Jesus. Just as God was moved when his Son suffered, he is moved when Jesus' followers are despised, rejected, and sometimes even tortured for being faithful to him. Truly, he suffers when he sees us cry out in pain.

Q: When I suffer, is this because God is punishing me for my sins?

A: Our heavenly Father is not mean but gentle and loving. Nevertheless, he is not permissive either. Sin is abhorrent to him, and he is not pleased when we engage in unrighteous behavior or dwell on wicked thoughts. Scripture reminds us of God's parental role toward us: "My child, do not regard lightly the discipline of the Lord, or lose heart when you are punished by him; for the Lord disciplines those whom he loves, and chastises every child whom he accepts" (Hebrews 12:5–6).

All suffering, however, is not the result of sin on our parts. Sometimes we are the victims of other people's evil actions or unfortunate circumstances. We may even be the target of people's hostility toward God. In fact, "if you endure when you do right and suffer for it," the apostle Peter tells us, "you have God's approval" (1 Peter 2:20). He went on to say just as Christ suffered for living righteously, we also will suffer when we follow in his footsteps (verse 21).

So suffering can be either the result of our sins or the consequence of our faith in Christ. With the former, it teaches how to live a godly life; with the latter, it identifies us as a true follower of Jesus. In either case, God will never allow us to suffer to the point that it breaks our spirit.

Q: Does God sometimes bring suffering into my life to teach me something?

A: Think of the times in your life you suffered most. Inevitably, once the suffering diminished, you were stronger, wiser, and more compassionate than before. God knows that sometimes the only way to teach us great life lessons is to give us the means to show what we are made of. And the only way we can show what we are made of is by being stretched, challenged, and forced to walk through the fire. As William Cowper once proclaimed, "God moves in mysterious ways His wonders to perform."

Without suffering, we would become weak and ineffective, never really knowing just how strong we are or how powerful our faith in God truly is. Suffering allows us to reveal our true selves and to live from a much deeper spiritual truth about who we are. Suffering tests us, and we either pass or fail.

If we fail, God will no doubt test us again and again until we get it right,

Tests and suffering are meant to make us grow and learn. "My brothers and sisters," James wrote, "whenever you face trials of any kind, consider it nothing but joy, because you know that the testing of your faith produces endurance; and let endurance have its full effect, so that you may be mature and complete, lacking in nothing" (James 1:2–4). When we finally "get" this, we can look at our suffering with new eyes and understand that it is an opportunity in disguise to prove our commitment to God.

Q: Does most or all suffering come from Satan?

A: Suffering occurs when something is not right— whether it is our body, a relationship, or a situation. Because Satan always seeks disorder in the world and in our lives, we could say he is the source of the suffering we feel or see. But then, in a way we are passing the buck, for much of the suffering we experience is because we have not done what is right before God. We are the ones sinning, and as

25

Christians we must take full responsibility for our sins and the suffering our behavior brings upon others and ourselves.

Many events occur in the world that bring great suffering, such as hurricanes and earthquakes. They are natural occurrences that are part of the way our planet is shaped, and they are not morally evil or Satanic. When we choose to live in the paths of tornadoes or close to earthquake faults, we do so with the knowledge that we are at risk. When something does happen, we cannot blame Satan for that natural phenomenon.

Other forms of suffering such as war, poverty, and crime are evils created by humans. People sin, and consequently, they, as well as others, suffer. Satan probably had some hand in tempting people to sin, but usually they don't need Satan to force them to sin. They go willingly and of their own accord.

Until we take the responsibility for our sins, we will never really understand why we are suffering. We will always believe what is happening to us is unjust, and invariably we will feel God does not care. It is easy to blame others for our failing (like what Adam did with Eve) or blame Satan (like what Eve did with the serpent). It is much more difficult to accept blame, but when we do, suffering will always be more bearable knowing God will hold us tightly and will wipe away our tears as a mother does with her hurting child.

Q: If God is all-powerful and unquestionably compassionate, why doesn't he stop the world's suffering or evil?

A: God *will* put an end to human suffering and evil, but he will do so in his own time. Who are we to question God's timing or why he allowed suffering and evil in the first place? They are questions that Job struggled with while he suffered, and the answer God gave were his own questions for Job, as well as for us: "Who is this that darkens counsel by words without knowledge? ... Where were you when I laid the foundations of the earth? Tell me, if you have understanding?" (Job 38:2, 4). In other words, how can we who are God's creations question the plans of the Creator with our limited knowledge, much less understand his plans?

God did not explain himself to Job, nor has he with any other person. He does not need to. He is God.

He is all-powerful and all-knowing. He alone knows the higher meanings behind every suffering and every evil perpetrated on humanity. God knows there is a deeper reality than the one we humans are able to perceive. He has the wisdom we do not, and he sees all when we can see only in part.

Nevertheless, through his Word, God tells us again and again that he will put an end to suffering and evil. This knowledge he does want to convey to us, for it gives us hope and strengthens our faith. When a mother delivers her baby, she endures terrible pain. But when she holds her baby in her arms, she forgets that pain and rejoices for the living gift she has received. God knows that we suffer for a time, but when it is over and we are with him in heaven, we will forget what we have suffered and enjoy the great blessings he has in store for us.

Q: As Christians, what should we do when we see suffering?

A: The best way to answer this question is to first ask, "What would Jesus do?" And then we should ask, "What things did he do that we can emulate?"

Of course, we do not possess the power to heal people the way he did, but we can demonstrate Jesus' compassion by providing physical, financial, and emotional aid however we can.

Because we have different talents and resources, we can help others in different ways. If we are in the medical profession, we can treat people with physical afflictions. If we are carpenters, we can build homes for the poor. If we are wealthy, we can relieve victims of natural disasters. If we are friends with someone dealing with an emotional crisis, we can provide counsel and comfort. We all have something to give, and what we can give God can use to alleviate the suffering of others.

When Jesus saw someone who was suffering, he felt deep compassion for that person and often he healed that person. We, too, can offer help and assistance to the best of our ability. Indeed, to reach out to another is the highest form of compassion, and that is what God would want of us as Christians. We cannot raise the dead, but we can certainly raise the spirits of those who suffer.

Q: As Christians, what should we do when we see evil?

A: Evil, like suffering, should bring out the best in us as Christians. But how can we be at our best as Christians? We need to once again think in terms of what Jesus might do when encountering evil. Although he did not raise an army to combat evil, he did stand up to it, exposing it for what it is in God's eyes. Whether evil showed itself as bigotry, hatred, or hypocrisy, Jesus never hesitated to condemn it, even when his words angered those with worldly powers.

Like our Lord Jesus, we must also recognize the true face of evil. There's a world of difference between a person who takes twisted pleasure in abusing and killing children and a person who promotes a different religion with sincerity and gentleness. We should not identify everything that does not agree with our Christian beliefs as instruments of evil. Nevertheless, those people and institutions that clearly manifest Satan's character need to be exposed and condemned.

All Christians can do something. Whether it be writing a letter to a political leader or corporate office, attending a town hall meeting to protest a bad law, fighting crime by starting a neighborhood watch group, raising our children to be loving beings, or working in our own lives to rid ourselves of hatred and racism, there is always something we can do to make the world a better place.

Because acts of kindness cancel out evil, the more kindness we can spread the better our world will be. When we see cruelty, we must stand up and speak out against it even if we are afraid of the repercussions. Jesus never stayed silent in the face of cruelty. If we see a crime being committed, it is our duty to tell the authorities. If we see oppression, we must take a stand against it. If we see hatred, we must counter it with love.

Evil may always be with us during our lifetimes, but that must never stop us from doing what is right, what is kind, and what is good. That is what Jesus did, and as Christians, it is what God expects us to do as well.

Q: When one of my friends suffers, what should I say or not say as a Christian to be helpful?

A: As Christians, we must always seek to lift the spirits of those who suffer, and the best way to do this is with honesty, kindness, and understanding. In other words, speak from the heart when in the presence of a friend who suffers. Tell them you love them and that you are there for them in whatever way they need a friend. Find a small way to make their life a little easier as they suffer, perhaps taking on some chores they are simply too weak or ill to handle.

Words are not as important as your loving presence and your compassionate spirit. Your friend will feel this love and caring, and they will respond to it. But if you feel you must say something, let them know that they are loved by God and that they have within them the power to receive God's merciful grace in times of need if they desire to do so. Pray with them if they are open to it, gently reminding them that they are God's beloved child and that he is there for them, just as you are. If they seem to be unresponsive, encourage them to seek outside help either at their church or through a doctor.

Do NOT ever say that their suffering is meaningless, trivial, or something that will "go away with time." Even though suffering does diminish with time, that is still an insulting thing to say to someone whose wounds are fresh and whose grief is deep. Instead, acknowledge their pain and grieve with them, never making them feel as though they should "buck up and get over it." Grief and mourning take time, and plenty of it. If they are angry at God, let them be. They will come to understand that their heavenly Father loves them and does not want them to suffer. But for now, God can take their anger. He will know what to do with it.

Christians committed to the teachings of Jesus will automatically behave in ways a true friend would—with love, compassion, empathy, and concern. That is what it means to be a Christian—to act like Christ, who was the most compassionate of all men and women. Be there to offer support and help, let them cry on your shoulder and tell you their fears, or just sit with them in total silence. Respond to their cues of how they can best be served by your friendship and your love. And then respond to them from the heart, letting God's love for them be expressed through you at all times.

CHAPTER THREE

Discovering God

What better relationship can a person have than to have an intimate relationship with God, the Creator of the universe! But, in order to have such a relationship, we must first know who God is and where we can find him. Discovering God is actually quite simple: He is right here before you, and he wants you to get to know him. He is not hiding from you, nor does he reveal himself to only a select few. He is waiting to embrace all of us with his love and mercy.

Q: I sometimes feel close to God when I am with nature. Does God show himself to us in the natural things of the world?

A: Look at a mountain, and you see God. Peek under a rock, and he is there, too. Walk through a field of white daisies, and there you will find him. In the solitude of nature, we are often able to hear the voice of God. "Ever since the creation of the world," said Paul, "his eternal power and divine nature, invisible though they are, have been understood and seen through the things he has made" (Romans 1:20). Nature is God's playground and our abundant playground as well; it is a place where we can truly commune with our Creator.

Even though we can find God in the noisy, busy city and the bustling suburb, it is much easier to hear God's voice in the quiet stillness of the natural world. Gone are the day-to-day distractions and stresses that normally assail us. Instead, in nature we forget the worries of our lives for a while and focus on God and his wonderful creation.

Q: What are the best ways I can find out about God?

A: The Bible describes many ways we can learn about God. Of course, the best way is to read about God in the Bible itself, which is filled with stories about how God interacted with men and women from the beginning of human history to the early days of the Christian church. Moreover, the life of Jesus told in four Gospel accounts provides clear impressions of what God is like.

Another effective way is through prayer. Jesus implored us to pray to our heavenly Father daily, and Paul added that we should pray without ceasing as if our very lives were a prayer of praise and thanksgiving to God (see 1 Thessalonians 5:17). When we pray to God, it's as easy as talking to a close friend, telling him our joys, sorrows, fears, and dreams. Prayer does not have to be a big, complicated chore, and it sure doesn't have to be perfect. It just has to come from the heart. God does not want our posturing and posing. He just wants us to be honest and open.

In addition to praying, we can read books by writers who have experienced God in their lives and have been faithful to his will. We can also seek out sisters and brothers in Christ who are filled with godly wisdom. Their stories and insights will surely inspire us as we learn how loving and compassionate is our heavenly Father.

Of course, a Bible-believing church will offer many opportunities to learn more about God. Whether it be in the worship service, a Sunday school class, or a retreat, there are many ways God is reaching out to you so you will get to know him better. At church is also an ideal place to learn.

Q: Does God have a personality with feelings and desires? What is he like?

A: "God is love" (1 John 4:16). Therefore, we can say he possesses all those qualities we equate with love. He is good and strong, wise and caring, merciful and forgiving. In fact, 1 Corinthians 13 provides an excellent portrait of what true love is—the very qualities that God has: "Love is patient; love is kind; love is not envious or boastful or arrogant or rude" (verse 4).

On the other hand, God says of himself, "I the Lord your God am a jealous God" (Exodus 20:5). This does not mean that God is envious of the adoration given to certain people or things. It does mean that he demands our singular devotion, which rightfully belongs to him as the Creator. Moreover, he knows that a life dedicated to him will be blessed with eternal peace and joy while a life dedicated to false gods will ultimately lead to disappointment and failure. Thus, his jealousy is a result of his deep concern for our welfare; it is a natural outpouring of his loving character.

Q: If God is love, what am I to think of all of those stories in the Bible where he seems wrathful? What am I to believe when I think he is being too harsh with me?

A: God's love is not restricted to a select group of people. He loves everyone who has ever lived, who is living now, and who will live in the future. "The Lord is," said the apostle Peter, "not wanting any to perish, but all to come to repentance" (2 Peter 3:9). The fact, however, is that many people have rejected his love and have turned to evil. Even those who have chosen to follow Christ have failed God at times. When wickedness occurs, the Lord, being a righteous God, cannot turn a blind eye to it; he must eradicate it lest it fatally poison the person or utterly pollute the populace.

God's reaction to evil in the world is often seen as overly severe. During those times in which men and women have given themselves to the dark forces of the world, the Bible has often shown God to be full of wrath. Yet, let us not forget that God is perfectly wise and that he knows how far he should go to combat evil at any given time. To do nothing at all would be to allow evil to thrive absolutely. To eradicate it is reserved for the day of judgment.

Remember when you were just a kid and your mom and dad disciplined you for doing something wrong? They may have punished you by grounding you, or taking away your television privileges, or giving you a time-out in the corner. It may seem to you that they were being mean, but later you realized that they were really trying to redirect you from doing bad to doing good. So it is with God. His discipline seems overly harsh but is actually God's wise hand guiding us back to the path of righteousness. In fact, if our parents had never disciplined us, we would have thought their permissiveness was uncaring and destructive for our lives. And this is how we would think of God if he allowed us to do whatever we wanted.

God is often seen as punishing and angry because he is the Father and we are often his wayward and ignorant children, stumbling our way through life and in much need of guidance and discipline. On our Christian path, we hurt ourselves and other people. We need rules, and we need guidance.

When we feel as though life is punishing us for something, often something we instigated or took conscious part in, we take out our anger on God because it feels as though he is the one punishing us for our sins. But if we are really honest with ourselves, we see that he is not punishing us but simply letting the consequences of our actions teach us the life lessons we so deeply need.

To think of God as a loving parent is to embrace every aspect of his love for us, which often comes in the form of tough love or strong discipline. It's always for our own good, though. For who should know better what we need to succeed than the one who created us in the first place?

Q: How can I be certain God loves me?

A: The simple fact that God made you means he adores you. Would you waste time creating something you did not love? God truly loves us, and he showed it by making us in his image.

Often it seems as though God does not care or that he has abandoned us, but if we are honest, we realize we were the ones who abandoned God. We get so caught up in our cares and worries that we forget to check in with him, and then we lose our connection to his loving Spirit, which is ever-present.

Consequently, we feel as though we have been cut loose from him to walk our path alone when the truth is that he is always standing beside us, waiting for us to recognize him. We feel abandoned and unloved just like a little kid who wants candy for breakfast and doesn't get what she wants.

When we sin, we turn away from God's love, and then we wonder where he went and why he betrayed us. But who betrayed whom? When we are anxious or afraid, we turn away from God's love, and then we wonder why we feel so alone and lonely. But who left whom?

All we have to do is turn around, and there God is, waiting with love and patience for us to snap out of it and get back on track. Now that's a loving Father.

God is love, and he loves us at all times. He loves us when we are happy as well as when we are sad. He even loves us when we sin or hurt others or ourselves. He loves us when we are nasty, mean, scared, stupid, or lazy. He shows his love to us every day by bringing us a new sunrise with all its opportunities to feel and express joy. Once we truly connect with God, we will never feel unloved again, and we will begin to "grow up" as Christians and act accordingly.

Q: Can God do anything? Are there no limits to his abilities?

A: The Bible tells us that with God all things are possible, even those things that seem utterly impossible to humans (see Matthew 19:26). Because he is all-powerful, all-knowing, infinite, and eternal, God can do everything, see everything, be everything, and create everything that's good. There is not one good thing he is not able to do, and thus, there are no limits to his powers and abilities.

Throughout the Bible there are examples of his supernatural actions. Time and again stories tell of a God who helps people overcome monumental dangers and tremendous obstacles and of a God who can bend and shape time and space and everything in between according to his will. When we look at the miraculous deeds God has done for his people, we realize that he is the ultimate superhero!

Even though God is all-powerful, he has not made us into robots or puppets. He has given us the freedom to walk the path we have chosen to walk, and that path might be the one he wants us to take or a path that goes against his will. He gives us the opportunity to exhibit our faith in Christ and grow into mature, righteous people.

This does not mean that our heavenly Father is not there for us when we desperately need him. He is always present and always willing and ready to help us when we call upon him. But we must be active participants in our own lives and cocreators with God of our destinies, and that requires us to understand that God's will may sometimes not be readily discernable. Things may not always be as they seem, and when it looks as though God is not able to do something for us, there is usually a deeper reason why.

Q: Does God know everything? Even the future? If so, does this mean that the future is already planned for me?

A: Wise and all-knowing, God knows and sees the past, the present, and the future. But this doesn't let us off the hook. Life is what we make of it, and even though God has set out a path for each of us as Christians to walk in glory, it is up to us not only to choose the right path but also to stay on the course for the long haul, even when the going gets really rough for us.

You could say that each of us has a specially appointed destiny, a future designed just for us that will bring us joy and fulfillment and that will make the best and highest use of our gifts and talents. Indeed, God knows that if we stick to his guidance and his will, we will realize our destinies as Christlike beings. On the other hand, we can choose to ignore God's guidance and create a totally different destiny than what God originally had in mind for us.

Look around you at all the unhappy, unfulfilled people in the world. They, too, have a destiny and a grand design for their lives, but because they refuse to follow God, they end up repeating the same mistakes over and over again, always wondering why God seems to bless so many others but not themselves. So they create their own destinies apart from God.

If we have the wisdom, courage, and discernment to take God's hand, we will certainly arrive at the destiny God has in store for us—and what a destiny that will be!

Q: What is the Trinity? How can a teaching that is deeply perplexing be vitally important?

A: The Trinity is a concept that every Christian should understand, not because they are supposed to, but because it is a wonderful concept that brings us even closer to understanding who God is.

In the Book of Deuteronomy, the children of Israel were told, "Hear, O Israel: The Lord our God, the Lord is one" (Deuteronomy 6:4 NIV). And the apostle Paul affirmed for Christians, "There is one God" (1 Timothy 2:5). That means that only one God exists. Both Jews and Christians believe in the Almighty God. And yet, some people accuse Christians of believing in many gods because we say the heavenly Father is God, his Son Christ Jesus is God, and the Holy Spirit is God. What we believe is that there is one God revealed to us in three persons: the Father, the Son, and the Holy Spirit.

A good analogy can be drawn by looking at the properties of an atom. An atom has a certain number of protons, electrons, and neutrons. All three together identify what the atom is. However, they cannot exist separate from each other and still be that atom. So, too, the Father, the Son, and the Holy Spirit together identify who God is, but they are not individual gods existing independent of each other.

Each person of the Godhead offers us a different view of the one God, and each serves a vital role in establishing and maintaining an intimate relationship with us.

Q: What is the Holy Spirit? And why do some Bibles call this the "Holy Ghost"?

A: The Holy Spirit or Holy Ghost is the third person of the Trinity. When Ananias tried to deceive the apostles, Peter said to him, "Why has Satan filled your heart to lie to the Holy Spirit? ... You did not lie to us but to God!" (Acts 5:3–4). Here Peter referred to the Holy Spirit as God, and in the King James Version, the reference is translated as "the Holy Ghost." The Holy Spirit and the Holy Ghost are one and the same; they're just different terms people have used to describe the third person of the Trinity.

Paul made a distinction between the three persons of the Godhead when he ended his letter to the

Christians in Corinth by blessing them with: "The grace of the Lord Jesus Christ, the love of God, and the communion of the Holy Spirit be with all of you." (2 Corinthians 13:13). Of course, it is through the grace of Christ and the love of God that we are saved and through the indwelling of the Holy Spirit that we are transformed into the image of Christ. The Holy Spirit has many important functions, and two of them are to teach us and protect us (see John 14:26; 17:11). In fact, Jesus said, "I tell you the truth: it is to your advantage that I go away, for if I do not go away, the [Holy Spirit] will not come to you; but if I go, I will send him to you" (John 16:7). So now the Holy Spirit abides with us, leading us to God's truths and teaching us Christ's righteousness.

Q: What are angels? Are they important? Do they still exist today?

A: From our earliest Sunday school days, we are taught about angels. Acting as go-betweens, these marvelous entities watch over us, guide us, send us messages, help us in times of need, and comfort us when we are sad or afraid.

47

The interesting thing about angels is that they existed before the creation of humankind. In fact, the creation story in Genesis does not tell us when and why God brought them into being. Angels are mentioned for the first time later in the Book of Genesis with no explanation about them as if their existence was a given. From this we can determine that angels, from the great and mighty archangels to the lesser beings that populate the heavens, have served as God's special envoys to humanity from the time they first comforted Hagar in the wilderness (see Genesis 16).

Two angels are prominently mentioned in the Bible. The angel Gabriel visited Mary and told her that the Holy Spirit would come upon her and that she would conceive a child, and "he will be called Son of God" (Luke 1:35). He was, of course, Jesus. Gabriel also appeared to Zechariah, the father of John the Baptist (see verses 8–20). Another famous angel is the archangel Michael, who has contended with the devil (see Jude 9), and at one point Michael and God's angels defeated Satan and his followers and cast them out of heaven (see Revelation 12:7–9).

Angels bring messages from God. They comfort those who are suffering. They empower God's people to perform great deeds of righteousness. They teach us about God and his truths. They mold our characters to be Christlike. And they wage a cosmic war against the forces of darkness.

Q: If God already knows what we need, what is the purpose of prayer?

A: Prayer is not just a technique for getting what we want from God, but it is a way of communing with God on a daily basis. When we pray, we open ourselves up to God and his loving presence. Whether or not we have anything we need to ask from him is secondary, especially since he already knows all about our innermost dreams and desires. The primary purpose of prayer is simply to talk with our heavenly Father.

As a Christian, your whole life should really be a prayer. Why wait until right before you go to bed to connect with God, when your life would be amazing and joyful if you kept that connection going all through the day and night? That's what Paul meant when he suggested we pray without ceasing (see 1 Thessalonians 5:17). Life itself should become our prayer, a constant asking and receiving of God's good grace.

Another great thing about praying, especially when we do have something we want or need, is that it helps get our minds and hearts focused on what we should desire. By putting our needs into words, we get to the heart of what we are looking for. We set aside the ego and turn to God to get to the essence of what we desire. Is it a good job we seek or more abundance and prosperity? Is it a spouse we want or more love in our lives in general? Is it leadership in the church or more power over others?

Christians actually don't need to ask for anything because if they live in Christ, God will always give them what they truly need. Nevertheless, God wants us to express what we are thinking and feeling. Our desires are important to him. When we talk about what is on our minds and in our hearts, we feel closer to God in the same way as when we share our most intimate thoughts and feelings with those we trust the most. And who can we trust more and have a better intimate relationship with than with God?

So pray if you need something, and pray if you don't need a thing. Pray if you are sad and fearful, and pray if you are excited and happy and filled with deep gratitude. Just pray and talk with God. Even though God knows your mind and your heart better than you do, he always likes to hear the sound of your voice.

Q: When I pray, do I pray to God the Father or do I pray to Jesus Christ?

A: In some church settings, you are told to pray to the heavenly Father in the name of Jesus Christ. In other church settings, there are no hard and fast rules about praying. In either case, pray to either God the Father or Jesus Christ when you are praying on your own. Since God the Father and Son are one, it probably does not matter to them whom you are addressing as long as you are talking with one of them. The important thing is to engage in the act of prayer itself and not worry so much about your technique as long as you are sincere and humble when you come before God.

Jesus did implore us to pray to God the Father, and his prayer of choice was what came to be known as the "Our Father" prayer. But then again, Jesus wasn't about to pray to himself, was he? If you feel a deeper, more personal connection to God by praying to Christ, then by all means do so.

Q: Do I really need to go to church to discover God? Maybe I can just have a relationship with God by myself.

A: Church attendance doth not a Christian make! In fact, many people go to church only to sin up a storm when they get home, thinking that they are absolved just because they placed a few dollars on the donation plate. It's as if they have dual personalities, the one they show at church and the one they show the rest of the world.

Jesus did not say the church building is the church. Instead, he said, "For where two or three are gathered in my name, I am there among them" (Matthew 18:20). In other words, the church is an assembly of people who have gathered together to worship God the Father and Jesus Christ his Son. Nevertheless, Jesus also understood the special feeling people get in a temple or holy place of worship and that within the quiet walls one could shed the cares of the outside world and join with other believers in communion with God.

A church building is not holy or special in and of itself. It is special because of what goes on within its walls. You do not need to go anywhere special to discover God. He is right where you are, closer than breath and nearer than your hands and feet. But there is something special that happens within a church, especially when you have found the right fit among the many churches that exist.

Although God doesn't just hang out in a church building on Sunday mornings, attending a church that inspires, empowers, and enlightens you will bring you much closer to God than you might ever imagine possible. It's a wonderful place where you can contemplate God, forget your cares, and connect with God in an environment that is specially created to bring about feelings of reverence and praise.

Once you find a church you love, become more than just an attendee. Become a member of its family. After all, what better place to meet, worship, and become friends with people just like you, striving to be the best Christians they know how to be?

Q: Why do people in churches seem openly
hypocritical? Why does God allow them to
be in his church when they discourage
others from going to church?

A: "It is common for those that are farthest from
God," Matthew Henry once said, "to boast
themselves most of their being near to the church."
Jesus also commented on the subject of hypocrisy
when he told his disciples not to be hypocrites when
they pray (see Matthew 6:5). He then referred to a
particular type of religious folks who worshiped in
the Jewish synagogues in such a way that showed
how pious they were. Of course, many of these
people have made themselves known in churches
since Christians have first gathered together.

We often wonder why God endures their presence
within the fellowship of believers. In fact, Jesus was
asked that very question, and he replied by telling a
parable about wheat and weeds growing together.
"No," he told the reapers, "for in gathering the weeds
you would uproot the wheat along with them. Let
both grow together until the harvest" (Matthew
13:29–30). In other words, God will wait until
judgment day to separate unrepentant hypocrites
from true believers.

As for Christians who are sincere in their faith in Christ, they are human and make mistakes, even long after they have accepted Christ. Sometimes we blow it, and God understands. At times, however, it is difficult for others to understand, even other Christians. If you see Christians in your church that discourage you, love them anyway. That's what Jesus would have done. If you see people in the church setting bad examples for those who are visiting your church, take it upon yourself to offer them a positive example of what a true Christian should be.

As we struggle to be better Christians, we will always come head to head with our own humanity and all the quirks and dysfunctions with which human beings are packaged. But as long as we keep "suiting up and showing up," the Holy Spirit will always be transforming us into the character of Christ.

CHAPTER FOUR

How God Made Me and What He Desires

*W*hen you look in the mirror, what do you see? What you see may be quite different from what God sees. Yet, if we see ourselves through God's eyes, we will have a far healthier view of ourselves. We will at once see our nobility as God's special creation and our frailty as creatures in need of God's protection. Taking time to have an honest look at ourselves from God's view can only be good for us.

Q: What does it mean to be "made in the image of God"?

A: Humans are exalted above all other creatures, for only humans among creative beings are blessed with the image of God. Not only do they have a lofty place in God's heart, but they also have a sacred responsibility not to diminish or tarnish God's glorious image within them. Instead, they are to exemplify God's character: that is, of compassion, love, and righteousness.

Despite the Fall (when Adam and Eve disobeyed God in the Garden of Eden) and despite our own failings, we still bear God's image. If we observe other creatures, we will note our uniqueness in that we possess special intelligence and creative artistic gifts, an eternal soul, and the singular capacity to worship the Creator. Although humans can engage in wickedness, we can also perform noble acts of self-sacrifice that reveal our unique connection to God, who has created us in his image.

※※

Q: Should Christians separate themselves from "the world"? If so, how do I do this? How do I know what things to avoid?

A: Jesus taught us to be in the world but not of the world. What he meant was that we should not separate ourselves from non-Christians while not succumbing to worldly temptations. In other words, we should be salt and light (a godly presence) in the world (see Matthew 5:13–16).

So how do we find that fine line between walking in this world and not falling into its temptations? Each individual is unique, and that goes for Christians as well. Therefore, we need to examine our own character and honestly determine what spiritual gifts God has given us and what our personal weaknesses are.

God gives everyone a particular spiritual gift, and it is our responsibility to use it wisely and effectively to further the kingdom of God. Some gifts are necessary within the church, but every Christian has a spiritual gift that can be of benefit to people in the world. If your gift is hospitality, then welcome strangers into your home. If your gift is mercy, then minister to others who need material or physical help. If your gift is evangelism, then share the gospel with non-Christians.

At the same time, Satan knows just what button to push when we step out of our Christian circle into the world. It might be materialism, pride, jealousy, pornography, or any number of ungodly things. It is wise, therefore, to put a healthy distance between you and that particular temptation. "Discipline yourselves, keep alert," said Peter. "Like a roaring lion your adversary the devil prowls around, looking for someone to devour" (1 Peter 5:8). So be on guard for those things in the world that can easily overpower you, and flee from them when they appear. But don't hide from the world; it needs the salt and light you can provide in Christ.

Q: What is sin?

A: When the Bible talks about sin, it could be referring to sin in general or to a particular sin. In general, sin is the condition humans are in because of the Fall. In our inherited fallen state, it is our nature to behave contrary to God's laws, pursuing self-centered pleasures and godless ambitions. God is either to be ignored or to be opposed. This is our sinful nature or just plain "sin." A particular sin is that which we think, feel, or do because of our sinful nature. It could be fantasizing about someone's spouse, harboring anger toward someone who has slighted us, or stealing someone's watch. The Bible gives us many examples and lists of things that displease God.

Another way we can determine what is sin is to ask ourselves what Jesus would do in any given situation. If we don't follow Jesus' example, it is a sin, for "He committed not sin" (1 Peter 2:22). Of course, if someone has passed away, we can't raise that person from the dead as Jesus had done. We can, however, show compassion to those who are grieving even if they ridicule our belief in heaven.

Still, we are human, and we will continue to offend, break laws, defy God's will, miss the mark, and do wrong until we enter the heavenly kingdom and become entirely transformed into the character of Christ. And if we are truly contrite, Christ's blood will cover all our sins so we will be acceptable in God's sight.

Q: If God made me a new person in Christ, why do I still do bad things?

A: Although we have been reborn as God's children and have the Holy Spirit dwelling within us, we still must live in a fallen world, filled with ungodly forces. God could make us immune to evil, but then we would be merely living out our lives like puppets. We would not sin, but we would not have the freedom to enjoy life either. Until God eradicates evil once and for all, this world will tug at us to do bad things, and sometimes we will give in.

The apostle John knew this reality, and that is why he wrote, "If we say that we have no sin, we deceive ourselves, and the truth is not in us" (1 John 1:8). But this reality need not discourage us, for John went on to say, "If we confess our sins, he who is faithful and just will forgive us our sins and cleanse us from all unrighteousness" (verse 9). Yes, even though we are Christians, we still stumble in this world, but Christ will always pick us right up as we continue to take the path God has planned for us.

Being a new person in Christ does not mean we are finished, done, and complete. It means we are a "work-in-progress." We are a masterful piece of art being shaped and molded until one day we will see ourselves as God sees us—perfect.

Q: Will I be judged for the things that I do in this life?

A: The good news that Christians preach is that Christ came to earth to atone for our sins. Unless we receive God's grace and devote our lives to Christ, however, God will judge us for the things we do during our lives. And since no one, except Jesus, has lived a sinless life, we will be found guilty. "There is no one who is righteous," said Paul, "not even one" (Romans 3:11). That's why each one of us needs Jesus to be our advocate before God. And those he defends, God pardons.

This is great news, but it doesn't get us off the hook entirely. Accepting Christ as our Savior does not mean we can sin whenever we want and still get a free ride into heaven. We must make every effort to follow the teachings of Christ. If we truly love God, we will want to do just that. We will fail now and then, but we will keep trying to please our Lord.

For believers, a kind of judgment comes here on earth, for who hasn't paid an immediate price for their sins? We often see the consequences of our behavior right after we commit the sin. The worst part of it is how we hurt others and let our Lord down. But such sins do not cost our entry into heaven or—worse—our fellowship with God.

Q: I want to be good, but it seems that more rules make me more rebellious. What can help my efforts to be good?

A: Paul struggled with that very issue. "I delight in the law of God in my inmost self," Paul told the Christians in Rome, "but I see in my members another law at war with the law of my mind, making me captive to the law of sin that dwells in my members. Wretched man that I am! Who will rescue me from this body of death" (Romans 7:22–24). The more Paul tried to do good, the more he wanted to do evil. It was as though God's laws were urging him to do wrong.

How many of us can identify with Paul? We're told not to do something, but thinking about it makes us want to do it even more. Our spirit is willing, but our flesh is weak, and the more we resist, the more it takes a hold of us until it finally overwhelms us. Rules then become a curse rather than guidelines on how we can live a godly life. Paul's solution is the answer he gives to his own question: "Who will rescue me from this body of death? Thanks be to God through Jesus Christ our Lord!" (verses 24–25). Why, Paul? "For the law of the Spirit of life in Christ has set you free from the law of sin and of death"

(Romans 8:2). What we couldn't do in our flesh, God's Spirit can do through us. On our own, we will invariably succumb to sin, but if we allow God to rule our lives, no temptation is too great for us.

There are many things that can help us be good. We can pray for guidance. We can sing praises to God. We can study God's Word and the words of mature Christians. We can fellowship with other believers. We can serve those who are in need. God provides many ways for us to keep away from sin's clutches and to live a righteous life.

Q: What is the "Golden Rule," and did Jesus teach it?

A: "In everything do to others as you would have them do to you," Jesus said, "for this is the law and the prophets" (Matthew 7:12). In other words, treat others in the same way you want them to treat you (see also Luke 6:31). What Jesus bid his followers to do has become known as the "Golden Rule."

Many people believe this teaching is not unique to Jesus, and, in fact, his instruction is based on the ancient Jewish law: "You shall love your neighbor as yourself" (Leviticus 19:18). Some also note Confucius's exhortation not to do to others what you do not want them to do to you. Although Confucius predates Jesus by several centuries, there is a profound difference in that Jesus is telling us what to do while Confucius is telling us what not to do; Jesus' directive is proactive while Confucius's is passive. Nevertheless, Jesus is still drawing upon God's earliest commands to the ancient Hebrews.

There is no situation you will ever encounter that cannot be made more positive, loving, and beneficial when this rule is applied. Wars and conflicts would be nonexistent. There would be no violence, no hatred, no poverty, and no crime if we all lived by this one rule. If we always treated others as we wanted them to treat us, everyone would be fed, clothed, and sheltered. Everyone would be appreciated, acknowledged, and cherished.

Jesus spent his entire ministry teaching this wonderful and powerful law. The Golden Rule summed up almost everything he believed in: caring for the sick, loving one's enemies, not judging or condemning others, spreading love and peace, and turning the other cheek. Indeed, it is all about empathy—putting ourselves in the shoes of another, walking their path for a while, and treating them as we would hope they would treat us. With faith in God and the Golden Rule, we can learn to live truly Christlike lives.

Q: Jesus said that I have to love my enemy, but how can I love someone I hate?

A: When Jesus told his followers to love their enemies, he noted that it is easy to do good to someone who has done good to you (see Luke 6:32–35). What makes God's people stand out in this world is that they express God's character, a god who "is kind to the ungrateful and the wicked" (verse 35). And guess what? We are the ones Jesus was talking about; we are the ones who were "ungrateful" and "wicked." Yet, God has been "kind" to us. Therefore, we are to "be merciful, just as [our] Father is merciful" (verse 36).

It's easy to love those who love us back, who are kind to us, and who treat us with respect. They press all the right buttons and rub us the right way. But what a challenge it is for us to do good to someone

who has wronged us! Remember when Jesus asked
God to forgive his executioners because they were
not aware of what they were doing? Jesus serves as
the perfect example of how we are to respond to
people who have hurt us and, in some cases, are out
to get us.

Loving the enemy is a challenge every Christian must
accept joyfully and wholeheartedly. It may not come
easily, or even naturally, but this challenge must be
overcome if we truly want to be ambassadors of
God in this world, where so much selfless goodness
is needed.

Q: Why are Christians baptized?

A: Reflecting the death, burial, and resurrection
of Jesus, baptism is a powerful and joyful ritual of
cleansing, rebirth, and renewal that rewards us with
a new life in Christ (see Romans 6:1–11). In other
words, we have become dead to sin and alive to
God in Christ Jesus.

Prior to Jesus' resurrection from the dead, baptism
was a Jewish ritual that denoted ceremonial

67

purification; people, particularly priests, and articles of clothing and furniture were cleansed through baptisms. John the Baptist was famous for calling his people to repent of their sins, and his baptisms were known as "baptisms of repentance."

Christian baptism expanded the Jewish purpose for baptisms. John himself explained the difference when he declared that Jesus "will baptize you with the Holy Spirit and fire" (Matthew 3:11). In other words, when we are baptized into Christ, we receive the gift of the Holy Spirit, who then dwells in our lives and transforms our character into the likeness of Christ. It should be noted that when John baptized Jesus, it was not to cleanse Jesus of any sins since Jesus was sinless. Instead, the Holy Spirit alighted on Jesus, anointing him for his earthly ministry.

To be baptized is to be welcomed into the family of those who place their faith and trust in Christ. It is one of the most blessed times in the life of a Christian.

Q: What does it mean to "worship" God? Can worship be enjoyable?

A: The word "worship" means "to pay reverence or homage to," and that is exactly what we do when we praise the Lord as our Creator and the provider of our salvation. We sing hymns, offer prayers, and recite Scripture, thanking and honoring him for his grace and mercy.

Worship should always make us feel good and happy because we are acknowledging the abiding love the Lord has poured into our lives. Think of the loud and infectious sounds of a choir singing hymns and clapping with joy. That is worship. But so also is staring in awe at a blooming flower or a majestic mountain and being grateful for your children, your spouse, or your job. So, too, is saying a blessing before each meal, thanking God for always providing for your needs. Worship can also be something as simple as smiling at the sunrise each morning and vowing to live the day with a loving heart and a giving spirit.

Paying reverent respect to God can come in just about as many forms as there are creative humans. Some worship with words in prayers of praise and thanksgiving, but others might feel more comfortable painting pictures to God or writing poems about his mercy, his power, and his grace. Do a dance if you feel the urge. Or bow down and kiss the sacred ground you stand on. Recite his many names, or bake him cookies and then give them to the neighborhood children. It is all worship if it is an expression of love and thanks for God.

Don't worry so much about how you worship. Just find your own special way to express your love and your respect for God. And don't be shy. He wants to hear from you.

Q: Why are there so many different churches in the world? Why isn't there just one church or denomination?

A: Human beings are a diverse lot. We all have our own preferences. Some like to attend large churches because they offer a wide range of programs and opportunities to serve; others like the intimacy of a small congregation because it's like an extended family. Some prefer a liturgical worship service; others are more comfortable in an informal church setting. It would be almost impossible to find one church that appeals to all people in all ways. That is why there are so many to choose from. Variety is the spice of life!

As Christians, we want to find a church that teaches us to walk in faith with Christ, and we want to meet others that we can share fellowship with. Most of all, we want to feel a deep connection with God, a real resonance with the message the minister or priest is delivering each week, and a feeling that we belong to this family of believers.

There's nothing wrong with trying different churches until you find the perfect fit for you and your family. God won't mind. After all, he is present everywhere, and that includes every church!

CHAPTER FIVE

Jesus Christ, the Son of God

*F*rom the time Jesus began his earthly ministry, people have tried to fashion his character and mission into what they wanted him to be and do. But who is this man and how did he affect human history in ways no other person ever has? The Bible explains much about him, but if you get to know him personally, you will learn even more about the Son of God.

Q: Why was Jesus called "the Messiah"? What does that mean?

A: The term *Messiah* is a form of the Hebrew word for "Anointed One." The Greek translation of this word is *Christos,* which is Christ in English.

We find the ritual of anointing throughout the Old Testament. Typically kings were anointed when they ascended to the throne. Priests also received anointing when they began their service, and sometimes prophets were anointed as well. The rite involved pouring oil on someone's head, possibly symbolizing the outpouring of God's Spirit upon that person. Anointing indicated that the king, priest, or prophet was divinely chosen to serve God in a particular way and that God would provide the power necessary to do the job.

King David was the first individual specifically called an "anointed one," but the term also applied to his descendants—all the kings who would follow in David's dynasty. "Great triumphs [the Lord] gives to his king," the psalmist exults, "and shows steadfast love to his anointed, to David and his descendants forever" (Psalm 18:50). Once the nation of Judah fell to the Babylonian army, there was great hope for a future "anointed one" who would restore the throne of David.

But Isaiah's prophecies take a different approach. The coming deliverer is seen as a servant as well as a king. "Here is my servant," the Lord says, "... my chosen, in whom my soul delights; I have put my spirit upon him; he will bring forth justice to the nations" (Isaiah 42:1). Many Old Testament prophecies seem to have at least two fulfillments, one in the immediate future and another in the distant future. Thus, Isaiah 45:1 specifically names the Persian king, Cyrus, as God's "anointed." Cyrus, in fact, allowed the Jews to return to their homeland. But as the prophecy unfolds, it's clear that a future "anointed one" would do far more than Cyrus could ever dream of doing. This coming servant would be "wounded for our transgressions, crushed for our iniquities" (Isaiah 53:5).

By the time of Jesus, the Romans were occupying the land of Israel. Many Jews looked for a Messiah, an "anointed one," to defeat the Romans and once again claim the throne of David. Others looked for more of a priestly character, who would lead a spiritual revival while doing away with the sin of the nation. In his way, Jesus did both.

While he allowed others to call him the Messiah (Matthew 16:18), Jesus shied away from using the term himself, perhaps fearing the misunderstandings it might cause. He let his actions testify to his anointing.

When he began his public ministry in the synagogue at Nazareth, Jesus read the words of Isaiah 61:1: "The Spirit of the Lord is upon me, because he has anointed me to bring good news to the poor. He has sent me to proclaim release to the captives and recovery of sight to the blind, to let the oppressed go free, to proclaim the year of the Lord's favor." Then he sat down and said, "Today this scripture has been fulfilled in your hearing" (Luke 4:18–19, 21).

Q: Why does the Bible say Jesus "was born of a virgin"?

A: The Gospels of Matthew and Luke are both quite explicit on this point: Jesus had a miraculous birth from a virgin mother. Matthew saw it as a clear fulfillment of a prophecy in Isaiah. "Therefore the Lord himself will give you a sign. Look, the young woman is with child and shall bear a son, and shall name him Immanuel" (Isaiah 7:14).

This is one of several Old Testament predictions with double fulfillments and that has caused some trouble for translators. Isaiah used the Hebrew *almah,* which is a common word for any young woman, whether a virgin or not. The immediate context of his statement involved a political situation that would soon be resolved. The king was extremely worried about it, and Isaiah wanted him to trust God for the outcome. As a sign of God's protection, Isaiah said, a young woman would have a baby and by the time that

75

child was old enough to know right from wrong, the king's enemies would be defeated. Other nearby passages make us think this "young woman" was Isaiah's wife and the child was his.

But sometimes reading the Old Testament prophets is like looking at a mountain range. You think you're looking at one mountain when there might actually be several peaks, miles apart. Isaiah gave a current-events prophecy to his king, which came true within five or ten years, but there was more fulfillment to come. That name—*Immanuel,* which means "God with us"—hints that another birth in the future will resolve far greater problems. In fact, two chapters later, Isaiah recorded a clearly futuristic birth announcement: "For a child has been born for us, a son given to us; authority rests upon his shoulders; and he is named Wonderful Counselor, Mighty God, Everlasting Father, Prince of Peace. His authority shall grow continually, and there shall be endless peace for the throne of David and his kingdom. He will establish and uphold it with justice and with righteousness from this time onward and forevermore" (Isaiah 9:6–7).

In the century before Jesus' birth, some Jewish scholars gathered to translate the Hebrew Scriptures into Greek. This version, known as the *Septuagint,* became the Scripture text used by many Jews throughout the Mediterranean world. When these scholars came to Isaiah 7:14, they chose the word *parthenos* (virgin) for *almah* (young woman). And so the birth of Jesus not only fulfilled Isaiah's prophecy that a Prince of Peace would be born to a young woman, but it also was the miraculous virgin birth that readers of the Greek Scriptures would expect.

Some modern scholars have used this discrepancy in words to cast doubt on the virgin birth. To be sure, any miracle boggles the modern mind. But the first and third Gospels report it with no apology. When the angel announced the coming birth, Mary's own mind was boggled: "How can this be, since I am a virgin?" (Luke 1:34). The angel merely explained that the power of the Most High would "overshadow" her. Joseph was obviously bothered by the apparent infidelity of his wife-to-be, but the angel assured him, "The child conceived in her is from the Holy Spirit" (Matthew 1:20). The New Testament clearly presents Jesus as the Son of God in a physical, as well as spiritual, sense.

Q: If Jesus was human, does this mean that he made mistakes?

A: That depends on what you mean by "mistakes." The incarnation of Jesus Christ is one of the great mysteries of the Christian faith. We believe Jesus was both human and divine, but we haven't worked out all the details. The apostle Paul wrote that Jesus didn't cling to his divine privileges, but "emptied himself, taking the form of a slave" (Philippians 2:7). We assume that he gave up his omnipresence. God is everywhere at once, but part of being human is to be bound in time and space, isn't it? Did he also give up being all-powerful or all-knowing? The Gospels show us occasions when Jesus displayed awesome power, and other times when he seemed to read minds, but were these special cases, or did he find some way to meld these divine traits into his humanity?

So, what kind of "mistakes" might Jesus make? When he was first learning arithmetic, would he ever mistakenly say that 3 plus 4 was 9? Learning the carpentry trade, would he ever cut one table leg too short? Luke said the young Jesus "increased in wisdom and in years [or in stature], and in divine and human favor" (Luke 2:52). We can assume that

Jesus went through the normal growing processes of any child, and thus he probably made some of the natural learning mistakes that we make when we are children.

When it comes to *moral* mistakes, however, it's a different story. In talking about Jesus, the writer of Hebrews said, "For we do not have a high priest who is unable to sympathize with our weaknesses, but we have one who in every respect has been tested as we are, yet without sin" (Hebrews 4:15). So Jesus, being human, understands our weaknesses, and he has been tested (or tempted) in the same ways we are, yet he did not sin.

The sinlessness of Jesus is an important theological point that the New Testament writers uphold. In the Jewish sacrificial system, a perfect lamb was offered. Peter said we are redeemed by "the precious blood of Christ, like that of a lamb without defect or blemish" (1 Peter 1:19), and later he said of Jesus, "He committed no sin, and no deceit was found in his mouth" (1 Peter 2:22).

Q: What did people see in Jesus that made them want to follow him?

A: You might say the Gospel of John is all about answering that question. Chapter after chapter, John shows us people considering the question of who Jesus is and whether they should follow him.

Some of Jesus' disciples had previously followed John the Baptist. Although John's baptism focused on repentance for sin, John said there was more to come. God would provide a sacrificial lamb to take away the world's sin. When Jesus came along, John declared, "Look, here is the Lamb of God!" and some from his retinue began following Jesus (John 1:37). One of these was Andrew, who ran to tell his brother, Simon Peter, "We have found the Messiah" (John 1:41). Another disciple, named Philip, told his friend Nathanael, "We have found him about whom Moses in the law and also the prophets wrote" (John 1:45). So it was clear from early on that Jesus' closest followers sensed his divine mission.

Soon Jesus was performing miracles, which convinced others to follow him. A religious leader named Nicodemus had a secret rendezvous with Jesus, saying, "Rabbi, we know that you are a teacher who has come from God; for no one can do these signs that you do apart from the presence of God" (John 3:2). Because of these "signs," plus the personal challenge Jesus offered in this meeting, it seems that Nicodemus became a disciple of Jesus.

From the upper crust of society in John 3 to the outcast in John 4, Jesus encountered many different people. The outcast in John 4 was a Samaritan woman by a well. He spoke to her of "living water," and he revealed some uncanny knowledge of her shady past. After her encounter with Jesus, she returned to the city, saying, "Come and see a man who told me everything I have ever done! He cannot be the Messiah, can he?" (John 4:29). Many townspeople went out to see Jesus. Later they told the woman, "It is no longer because of what you said that we believe, for we have heard for ourselves, and we know that this is truly the Savior of the world" (John 4:42).

Apparently, Jesus had some who followed for the wrong reasons. After he miraculously fed a crowd of thousands, people flocked around him. "You are looking for me, not because you saw signs," he admonished them, "but because you ate your fill of the loaves" (John 6:26). When his teaching became more challenging, many casual followers drifted away. At one point Jesus turned to his 12 most loyal disciples and asked, "Do you also wish to go away?" Peter replied, "Lord, to whom can we go? You have the words of eternal life. We have come to believe and know that you are the Holy One of God" (John 6:67–69).

The testimony of those who chose to follow Jesus makes it clear that he had a powerful one-two punch. His teaching was unique and insightful and entertaining as well. His quips and stories make us laugh today, and no doubt he delighted crowds back then. But he also taught "as one having authority" (Matthew 7:29), something the people weren't getting from other teachers.

Yet, Jesus backed up his teaching with works of healing and other signs of divine power. He touched rich and poor alike, the righteous and the sinful. This fit with his recurring message of God's kingdom as a place run not on a merit system but on the mercy and forgiveness of the Father.

Q: In church people have a ceremony called "The Lord's Supper." What is this, and why did Jesus start it?

A: Various denominations hold different views on what the meaning of The Lord's Supper is, how to observe it, and what really happens when they do, but they all agree on how it started. The night before his crucifixion, Jesus celebrated a Passover meal with his disciples in an upper room in Jerusalem. This ritual, commemorating the Israelites' miraculous escape from Egypt, has been observed by devout Jews throughout the centuries. Each element of this meal—the meat, the bread, the vegetables, even the dip—carries a special meaning. At this "Last Supper" with his disciples, Jesus gave the bread and wine an entirely new meaning.

During the meal, Jesus took some bread and broke it. Passing it to his disciples, he said to them, "This is my body, which is given for you. Do this in remembrance of me" (Luke 22:19). After supper, he took a cup of wine and shared that as well, saying, "This cup is the new covenant in my blood. Do this, as often as you drink it, in remembrance of me" (1 Corinthians 11:25).

After Jesus rose from the dead and ascended into heaven, the disciples obeyed Jesus' command to "do this in remembrance of me." It's unclear exactly how often they did this. Some suggest they just had their annual Passover meal with Jesus in mind. Others see a daily observance mentioned in Acts 2:46: "Day by day ... they broke bread at home and ate their food with glad and generous hearts." It's more likely that the first Christians observed a weekly Sabbath meal, at which they took bread and wine while remembering Jesus' words.

By receiving the elements of Communion, the believer acts out the receiving of God's grace and forgiveness, which is offered through the body and blood of Christ. Was this what Jesus had in mind when he started the tradition? Perhaps. Obviously he was starting with a symbolic meal—the Passover—which celebrates the deliverance of God's people. He was announcing a "new covenant" between God and his people, one that would deliver them from the power and penalty of sin and death. His own broken body and shed blood would establish that new covenant, and a new community would be formed, a community of those who relied on Jesus' sacrifice for their own deliverance.

Q: What is "The Lord's Prayer"? And why do Christians say it so often?

A: "Lord, teach us to pray," Jesus' disciples asked him (Luke 11:1). He responded with a prayer that Christians have used as a model ever since. "The Lord's Prayer" appears in slightly different forms in Matthew and Luke, and different churches use a few different words or phrases, but the bulk of it is just what Jesus shared with his followers:

Our Father, who art in heaven
Hallowed be thy name.
Thy kingdom come,
Thy will be done
On earth as it is in heaven.
Give us this day our daily bread,
And forgive us our trespasses [or debts]
As we forgive those who trespass against us [or our debtors].
And lead us not into temptation,
But deliver us from evil;
For thine is the kingdom, and the power, and the glory forever. Amen.

Many Christians see this prayer as an outline for personal prayer. We begin with praise while praying for God to advance his kingdom on earth. Then we present our personal needs and confess our sins (as we open our hearts to forgive others). We ask for spiritual strength and then end again with praise. All of these components are found in other biblical prayers. Jesus pulled them all together in this example.

Q: Why did Judas betray Jesus?

A: This question is the stuff of novels. In fact, many fiction writers have tried to answer this very question, sometimes portraying Judas Iscariot as a frustrated revolutionary or a disillusioned fanatic. The door is open for all sorts of literary speculation because the Bible simply doesn't tell us why Judas betrayed Jesus.

The only clue we have about Judas's character is from John, who describes a scene in which Judas complained about the expensive perfume a woman poured on Jesus' feet. Surely it could have been sold, Judas contended, and the money given to the poor. John added his own editorial analysis: "He said this not because he cared about the poor, but because he was a thief; he kept the common purse and used to steal what was put into it" (John 12:6).

This suggests that the motivation for the betrayal might have been plain old greed. Thirty pieces of silver was not a fortune, but it still amounted to a month's wages for a common laborer. And Jesus had talked openly about the doom awaiting him on this trip to Jerusalem. Judas may have figured that Jesus would be arrested anyway, so why not make some money?

There's one other line of modern thought concerning Judas: the idea that God needed Judas to betray Jesus and used him for this purpose. Yes, Jesus seemed fully aware of Judas's intentions, predicting his betrayal and dismissing Judas from The Last Supper to "do quickly what you are going to do" (John 13:27). Even when Judas showed up with soldiers in the Garden of Gethsemane, Jesus said, "Friend, do what you are here to do" (Matthew 26:50).

Nevertheless, Luke wrote that "Satan entered into Judas" (Luke 22:3), and the Gospel writers held him fully responsible for his actions. Apparently he held himself responsible as well because he tried to return the money to the priests and, in remorse, went out and hanged himself (Matthew 27:3–5).

Q: Did Jesus' own people turn against him?

A: Yes, some Jewish leaders orchestrated Jesus' execution. Those particular leaders saw Jesus as a threat to a religious system that they controlled. On numerous occasions he had criticized them for hypocrisy, greed, and power-grabbing. He had also flouted their laws regarding work on the Sabbath day. While he was rather careful not to make personal claims that would be considered blasphemy against God, other people accused Jesus of such claims. The leaders also resented Jesus' popular appeal among the Jewish people, and they feared that an uprising of the common folk would bring the wrath of Rome down on all of them.

This latter fear prompted them to find a way to do Jesus in. Only the Romans could legally exercise capital punishment, and the Romans wouldn't care about a charge of religious blasphemy. But hadn't Jesus often talked about a "kingdom"? If he was promising to set up a new kingdom, why, that would be treason against Rome! First, these Jewish leaders had their own secret trial, finding Jesus guilty of blasphemy. Then, they handed Jesus over to the Roman governor, Pontius Pilate, on the charge of sedition against Rome.

Did the common people turn against Jesus? Probably not in any major way. Some have noted that crowds hailed Jesus' entry into Jerusalem on Palm Sunday, and days later they yelled, "Crucify him!" But were these the same people? It's more likely that these Jewish leaders planted their lackeys in the Good Friday crowd.

Be very careful about blaming the Jews for Jesus' death. Throughout history, this idea has stimulated atrocious acts on the part of so-called Christians. The truth is that many Jews followed Jesus, who was a Jew himself. His first disciples were Jewish, and the early church was primarily Jewish for its first few decades. An especially corrupt Jewish leadership and a very cruel Roman regime engineered the crucifixion. More importantly, the New Testament makes it quite clear that *our* sins put Jesus on the cross. All of us, Jews and Gentiles alike, are responsible for Jesus' death, which Jesus chose to do because of his love for each one of us. And we all can receive the mercy that flows from Jesus' ultimate sacrifice on the cross.

Q: What happened when Jesus died on the cross?

A: "Christ crucified" is the core of the gospel message (1 Corinthians 1:23), so it's no surprise that all four Gospels report the events in detail, and the rest of the New Testament explains its spiritual meaning.

Jesus was arrested in the Garden of Gethsemane at night and brought to trial before the Sanhedrin, the Jewish ruling council. Jesus' friends in the Sanhedrin, such as Nicodemus and Joseph of Arimethea, were not informed of this meeting. Jesus was charged with blasphemy, and because of misleading testimony, Jesus was convicted and then handed over to Roman soldiers. On the morning of Good Friday they brought him before the Roman governor, Pontius Pilate, with a charge of sedition against Rome. Pilate found no guilt in Jesus and tried to pass the buck by remanding him to King Herod of Galilee, Jesus' hometown. Herod was in Jerusalem for Passover, and after talking with Jesus, Herod sent him back to Pilate. When Pilate offered to release a prisoner for the holiday before a crowd outside his palace, the loudest yelled for the bandit Barabbas to be freed instead of Jesus.

And so Jesus was condemned to be crucified on a cross. He was forced to carry a cross beam outside the city walls to the place of execution, known as Golgotha or Calvary. There, his hands were nailed to the crossbeam, which was hoisted onto a pole or tree. His feet then were nailed to the pole or tree. Placed there about noon, he hung in agony for three hours.

The Gospels record seven sayings Jesus made from the cross: forgiving his tormentors; putting his mother Mary in the care of the disciple John (and vice versa); comforting a thief who was crucified beside him; asking for something to drink; questioning why God had "forsaken" him; saying, "It is finished"; and committing his spirit to the Father.

The Gospels record a number of startling occurrences at the moment of Jesus' death, around 3 P.M. The sky grew dark. The earth shook. A veil in the temple, marking off God's most holy dwelling, was torn from top to bottom. Matthew suggested that bodies came out of their graves and that these people later walked around town (though some scholars say Matthew might have been focusing on a spiritual meaning).

Scripture doesn't tell us what happened to Jesus' soul while his body lay in the grave. He did tell the thief, "Today you will be with me in paradise," but paradise could be a generic term for the afterlife. There's an ancient tradition called the "Harrowing of Hell" that says Jesus stormed the devil's domain and rescued the souls held hostage there. We find hints of this in 1 Peter 3:19 and the Apostles' Creed.

And that is precisely the spiritual impact of the cross, the rescuing of lost souls. Peter wrote that Jesus "bore our sins in his body on the cross" (1 Peter 2:24). If you focus on the physical agony of the crucifixion, you're missing the main meaning. The penalty for sin is death—spiritual separation from God—and Jesus paid that penalty on the cross. In a phrase turned by ancient monks, Jesus "gave death to Death through death." Paul wrote that God was "making peace through the blood of his cross" (Colossians 1:20). Thus, we are "dead to sin," and because Jesus rose three days later, we are "alive to God" (Romans 6:11).

Q: If Jesus was resurrected from his grave, where is he today?

A: The New Testament is adamant that Jesus was physically raised to life, but his body had some strange new properties. He could suddenly appear in rooms and disappear just as quickly, and yet he wasn't a hologram. Jesus ate breakfast on the shores of Galilee, Mary hugged him, and Thomas touched his wounds. Some believe Jesus' resurrected body was the "imperishable" body that Paul said we'd all receive upon Jesus' return (1 Corinthians 15:52, some versions call it "incorruptible").

After 40 days of teaching his disciples, Jesus ascended into heaven. Does he still have his imperishable body now, or is he in some spiritual, bodyless realm? Any answer would be guesswork.

We do know that many Scripture passages speak of Jesus "sitting at the right hand of God" (see Ephesians 1:20; Colossians 3:1). That is a position of responsibility: Any ancient ruler would have his most trusted minister at his right hand. Several verses refer to the power Christ wields from that position. Peter said Jesus "has gone into heaven and is at the right hand of God, with angels, authorities, and powers made subject to him" (1 Peter 3:22). Paul added that Jesus uses that position to intercede with the Father on our behalf (Romans 8:34).

Q: What does it mean to "have faith" in
Jesus?

A: The English word *believe* is too weak to
capture the full meaning of the biblical idea. It helps
to use other terms, such as *trust, rely on,* or *have
faith in.* As we encounter this concept in Scripture,
it appears to have two aspects: mental and active.
We believe that something is true, and then we act
on that belief.

The Book of Hebrews announces that it's impossible
to please God without faith, "for whoever would
approach him must believe [1] that he exists and
[2] that he rewards those who seek him" (Hebrews
11:6). We've added those bracketed numbers to
point out the twofold nature of belief. We believe
God exists—that's a mental affirmation—but we
also trust that it's worthwhile to seek a relationship
with him, *and so we do*—that's action. The many
examples of biblical heroes in Hebrews 11 confirm
this. They acted on their faith in God.

Some modern folks put too much weight on the first
part and too little on the second; that is, they push
the mental belief in a particular theology, but they
underplay the value of personal action. It's not

enough just to have the proper mental ideas about God and Jesus. As James says, "Even the demons believe—and shudder" (James 2:19). No, faith in Jesus involves an active response.

The Bible speaks of this response several ways. "Repent, and be baptized," thundered Peter at Pentecost (Acts 2:38). That means sorrow for sin and a commitment to a new way of life, perhaps even involvement in a church. Paul said, "If you confess with your lips that Jesus is Lord and believe in your heart that God raised him from the dead, you will be saved" (Romans 10:9).

Don't get the idea that you have to follow a certain formula or perform certain deeds. Faith means trusting in God's grace, not in our own merits. And so the response of faith might be as simple as calling "on the name of the Lord" (Romans 10:13).

So, yes, read the Bible and believe that Jesus is the Messiah, that he died on the cross, and that he rose from the dead. But then grab those truths for yourself. This Messiah can set *you* free, he died for *your* sins, and he rose to give *you* new life.

It's like a chair. You can *believe* that a chair is well-made, that it's sturdy and dependable. But you don't really have *faith* until you sit on it. The same is true with your faith in Christ.

Q: Is Jesus the only path to God?

A: Jesus said he was, and the early church preached it. "I am the way, and the truth, and the life," he told his disciples. "No one comes to the Father except through me" (John 14:6). As Peter preached before the same council that condemned Jesus, he said, "There is salvation in no one else, for there is no other name under heaven given among mortals by which we must be saved" (Acts 4:12).

This is not a popular notion in modern times. We are taught to show respect for all religions, and many feel that this means all religions must be equally true. But Jesus didn't leave us that option. He claimed to be the only way.

This doesn't mean that Christians are better than everyone else, morally or intellectually. We haven't done anything to earn our access to God. We are merely sinners who have accepted the sacrifice Jesus has offered. We have no right to brag.

And this doesn't mean that all other religions are devoid of wisdom. When the apostle Paul visited the philosophers of Athens, he commended them for one particular pagan shrine, and he quoted local poets regarding their ideas about God (Acts 17). In fact, he said that people can figure out many truths about God by observing creation. "Ever since the creation of the world his eternal power and divine nature, invisible though they are, have been understood and seen through the things he has made" (Romans 1:20).

So various religions have valuable insights about the Creator, creation, and humanity. Nevertheless, the ultimate question is this: *How do we get past the sin problem and restore our relationship with God?* The Christian answer is "We can't, but God can." He has provided a way to pay for our sins and achieve reconciliation with God by becoming one of us in the person of Jesus Christ and by dying in our place.

Imagine that you're trapped in a burning building. All the exits are blocked. You sit there, desperately trying to figure out a way to escape from the fire when a firefighter breaks into the room. "Follow me," he says. "I can get you out of here."

What do you do? Do you say to the firefighter, "Well, actually I think there are several ways out, which are all equally valid"? Of course not! You take the exit route that's offered.

That's the Christian gospel. Sin puts us in a burning building, and we are powerless to save ourselves. There are no exits. We need help from the outside. Fortunately, Jesus breaks through and says, "Follow me to safety."

If we trust that Jesus speaks the truth, we won't look for any other way for help. We won't need to. Jesus has saved us.

CHAPTER SIX

Christianity and Other Religions and Traditions

*D*o all religious paths end at the same mountain peak? Many in our society say they do, and the general public seems to think they do. Yet, how can that be so if the goal of a Hindu is to become one with the cosmic universe and the goal of a Buddhist is to become extinct? If all religions essentially teach the same things, why do Jews and Muslims believe Christians are heretics for claiming Jesus to be God? The fact is that the major world religions and traditions have very different sets of beliefs about God, the human soul, and Christ.

Q: What makes Christianity different from the other major religions of the world?

A: Back in the early 1970s, you might have heard someone say, "I don't believe in religion, but I have a relationship with Jesus Christ." That might sound strange, but it is actually the essence of the Christian faith. When we analyze Christianity as a religion and compare it to other religions, we can miss out on its heart. Although Christianity does have a code of conduct, it is not about following rules. Although it has some great ideas, it is not a set of philosophies about life. Jesus said some brilliant things, which we embrace, but Christianity really isn't even about admiring those teachings. Christianity is all about the relationship we have with Christ and, through Christ, with God. This relationship goes on whether we follow the rules or not, whether we sin or not, whether we understand the teachings of Jesus or not. It is a commitment to a person rather than a religion.

Nevertheless, Christians tend to be religious people. Because of our relationship with Jesus, we try to do the things that please him. Because we love him, we hang on his every word. We practice the religion of Christianity as a result of our relationship with God, not as a way to reach him.

And so we come to this business of comparing religions. Lining up with the other great religions of the world—Judaism, Islam, Hinduism, and Buddhism—Christianity has some good things to offer. But still, for the most part, Christians do not become Christians because Christianity is a better religion. We enter the Christian faith because we find Christ there.

This emphasis on relationship makes Christianity sort of the "unreligion," setting it apart from others. Most other religions offer some sort of relationship with God, but that's the endpoint, not the starting line. We are generalizing here, of course, but in most other faiths, peace with God is the reward for a religion well practiced. With Christianity, we see Jesus at the beginning, saying, "Trust me. Now let me show you how to live."

Simply put, the difference between Christianity and other world religions is Christ. Historically, Christianity is Judaism with the addition of Christ. Like Muslims, we believe in one God, who cares how we act. But unlike Christians, Muslims view Christ as only a prophet. Christ for us is more than a prophet—he is the Savior who demonstrated God's love and forgiveness by dying for a wicked world. Like Buddhists, we resist the pull of the material world, but we dare to trust in a flesh-and-blood Redeemer whose suffering paid for our sins. You could point out differences in worship styles and world views, but the ultimate distinction of the Christian faith is Jesus Christ.

Q: Can all of the religions of the world be true at the same time?

A: Many people in our society have the idea that all religions are basically the same. Don't all "religious people" believe in God and try to be good? Maybe so, but how do you define God and how do you define good?

Muslims believe there is one God. Hindus believe there are many. Jews believe God is the Creator with an existence outside the created order. Some Eastern religions hold that God is within creation, and some would say the world itself is God. Can it all be true? Some groups—like Muslims, Orthodox Jews, and Mormons—place restrictions on foods that can be eaten. Other groups believe it's wrong to place such restrictions. Some religions espouse violence for a good cause, while others oppose violence in any form. Can all these groups be right?

Some folks get around these discrepancies by saying your religion is true "for you." You can worship whatever God you want, whatever works for you. And so religion becomes like a diet plan. If one plan stops working, try another plan.

That would make sense if your relationship with God was all about you. Many people treat religion that way—it's just another self-improvement method; you choose a religion that makes you a better person. But in that case, aren't you sort of "creating" God? And what kind of real power could that God possibly have?

But if there really is a Creator who made this world and everything in it, including you, wouldn't it make sense that this Creator has a particular identity? That is, wouldn't there be some qualities that this Creator has and other qualities the Creator doesn't have—whether or not you want it that way? The point is, it's not a matter of your choice. Once you choose to believe in a divine being who is greater than you are, worship becomes a matter of figuring out what the reality of this being is, rather than selecting whatever works for you.

So it's not just a matter of personal taste. There is an objective reality of God that the various religions of the world have tried to explain. Some religions, like Christianity, believe the Creator has communicated truth to people through prophecies and Scriptures. Perhaps God has communicated different things to different cultures at different times. It would be nice to believe everyone has a piece of a much larger truth, but sometimes there is direct conflict between the teachings of different religions. Did God create the world? Is there only one God? Is Jesus the divine Messiah? Will we live after we die? Some religions say yes and others say no. On these matters, it is only logical to conclude that some religions got it right and others got it wrong. That's not being proud or intolerant but just being sensible.

Q: How can I decide which religion to follow?

A: You want to ask of any religion, "Does it explain things in a way that makes sense?" Every religion has a kind of story to it, a way to understand the world, ourselves, and the supernatural. Does this story jibe with your own instincts? Does it answer your questions? Does it speak to your heart? Does it seem true?

But here's an even more important question: "Will this religion help me know God?" Philosophers have talked about a "God-shaped vacuum" inside us. We long to commune with our Creator, and we feel empty when we can't. Religions can bring order to our lives with their rules and traditions. They can inspire us with their stories and their portrayals of saintly people. But if they don't put us in touch with the divine, they're missing something crucial about our relationship with God.

The apostle Paul used an interesting term to refer to the Jewish religion. While he maintained that no one could keep the Jewish law perfectly enough to meet God's high standards, he said, "The law was our schoolmaster to bring us unto Christ" (Galatians 3:24 KJV). The old English translators used the word "schoolmaster," but the Greek word really refers to a household servant whose responsibility it was to take a child to school. The Jewish law has great value, Paul said, because it shows us how much we need a Savior like Jesus.

If you're seeking the right religion for you, that's a good thing to pay attention to. Does this religion lead me into a right relationship with God? That's something you should demand of any religious faith you might eventually follow, including Christianity.

Q: I want to respect other people's religions, but how do I do this if I think that their beliefs are wrong?

A: Imagine that your good friend Sally has gone off to Las Vegas and married a man you think is totally wrong for her. How will you treat her? She's still your friend. And how will you treat her new husband? You should treat him with respect because Sally has chosen him. You may never change your opinion of him, but you won't be carping about him.

It's a similar case when a friend chooses a religion you disagree with. You don't have to accept that religion as true, but your respect for your friend spills over to the friend's choices. If your friend asks your opinion, you should answer honestly, but it's not helpful to keep talking about how misguided your friend's religious choices are.

Chances are, even a religion you disagree with will have some aspects you can affirm. You might choose to focus on those aspects. But here's another thing you can do: Encourage your friend to seek God, whether in that religion or outside of it. Most people follow a religion as a way to understand and worship God. That's a good thing. You might disagree with the answers that a particular religion offers, but you can still support your friend's desire to know God better. So, ask about your friend's religious experience. That is, keep the focus on the basic question: "Is your religion helping you to know God better?"

This might yield some positive discussions that enrich your own understanding of God as well as your friend's.

Q: Am I really being intolerant when I regard other beliefs as false?

A: Sometimes truth has different flavors, like ice cream. Is God loving or demanding? Yes, and yes. Both can be true. So maybe one religion emphasizes one aspect while another faith focuses on the other. They can learn from each other. Is God "beyond" or "within"? Probably both are true. If you were to insist that chocolate is the only right flavor and pistachio was totally wrong, you would be an obnoxious boor. The same is true of some matters of religion. Being far greater than we are, our Creator can keep surprising us. For us to insist that our emphasis is perfectly right and everyone else's is wrong is being intolerant.

However, there are some yes-or-no questions in religion. Is Jesus the Son of God? Did he rise from the dead? Does God care how we behave? Can people find their own way to peace with God? These questions are less like ice cream and more like math. Two people can hold different positions, but both can't be right. What is two plus two? One says four, another says seven. Both are very sincere, but one is wrong. I can still be friends with you if you have the wrong answer, but I don't want you doing my taxes.

It's not always easy to know the difference between these two types of questions, and so we should be careful in religious discussions. The way of Christ is not only truth but also love and humility. Too many of us fight for the truth of Christ with a proud and hateful spirit. This does not please him.

But love doesn't mean automatically accepting all points of view as equally true. It does mean listening to others and treating them with respect. The Golden Rule applies here. How would you like others to deal with your beliefs? You'd like them to give you a hearing and to consider the points you make. You owe the same treatment to others.

Q: Should I try to convert them to my beliefs?

A: Let's work on terminology first. Trying to convert people sounds like you're remodeling your basement. The truth is, there's only so much you can do. It is God who woos people and redeems them. And it's not necessarily your beliefs they need to convert to. Who cares whether or not they agree with you about everything? They need to meet Jesus. So maybe the question is: Should I try to introduce people to Jesus?

Sure, we're being picky, but our words affect the way we think, and great damage has been done by well-meaning Christians who weren't thinking properly about this process. If you set out to "convert" people of other religions "to your beliefs," you won't find much success. Essentially you're saying, "Everything you believe is wrong. I've got it right. Be like me." Even if you do win some conversions, it might be just an exchange of religious symbols. The dynamic presence of Christ might get lost in the transaction.

But introducing people to Jesus? That's a worthy concept. The word "evangelism" means telling people the good news of Jesus—the news that God loves them and wants to know them, the news that Jesus has paid their debt.

It's amazing how little the New Testament talks in terms of "winning souls" and "converting the lost." Yes, Paul was a missionary, and he sometimes wrote about his own work like that, but rank-and-file Christians are urged to take a broader approach. We are to shine like lights in a dark world. "Let your speech always be gracious, seasoned with salt," Paul writes, "so that you may know how you ought to answer everyone" (Colossians 4:6).

It seems as if our lives should shine so radiantly with the presence of Christ that people will ask us what's going on. When they do, we should be ready. Peter writes, "Always be ready to make your defense to anyone who demands from you an accounting for the hope that is in you; yet do it with gentleness and reverence" (1 Peter 3:15–16).

Get that? Gentleness and reverence. You're not clobbering people until they accept your beliefs. You are gently explaining the hope that shines through you while showing respect to your listeners and reverence for the work that the Holy Spirit can do in their hearts.

So, yes. Try to introduce people to Jesus. Don't be deterred if they follow another religion. You have good news to share, and you would be remiss if you kept it a secret. Yet, in a sense of gentleness, you might want to let the light of Christ shine silently in your life for a while. Just be ready when they ask you about it. In the words of St. Francis, "Preach the gospel at all times. When necessary, use words."

Q: What can I learn from other religions?

A: The New Testament says that the basic nature of God can be understood from the universe he created (Romans 1:18–20). Some scholars call this "general revelation." Christians also believe God has communicated in a special way through the Bible (1 Peter 2:21). Christianity has developed through the centuries, based on the special revelation of the Scriptures, but many other religions and philosophies have been built on general revelation. And so there is a lot of truth to be found in some of these other religious faiths.

In addition, we can admire the dedication shown by adherents of other religions. Some of them have

forms of worship or prayer that we might use
as well. For example, we might learn from the
meditative practices of the Buddhists. This is very
much an inward religion, but we could adopt some
of their methods for quieting the body and mind.
The Bible says, "Be still, and know that I am God!"
(Psalm 46:10). We can meditate on the God who
lives both within us and beyond us.

In general, Muslims have a commitment to their faith
that Christians could emulate. Prayer is a regular
feature of their lives, and they seek to please God in
their choices of food and clothing as well. Too often,
our spiritual devotion becomes an optional factor
in our lives, easily dismissed when we get busy.
While we hold a trust in the grace of God and the
supremacy of Christ that Muslims don't have, we can
learn from their level of devotion.

Hinduism maintains that the material world is
illusion. They seek to transcend it. While Christianity
sees the physical world as a good thing created by
a good God, we also are warned not to be too
devoted to material wealth and pleasures. We can
appreciate the Hindu sense of the spiritual.

Nature religions, including some Native American
faiths, place a high value on the earth itself. As

Christians, we want to worship the Creator more than the creation, but we also see ourselves as stewards of the earth. We can learn a healthy appreciation of the natural world.

Q: How is a church different from a synagogue? A mosque? A Buddhist or Hindu temple?

A: In the New Testament, "the church" never refers to a physical building. It always means the group of Christians who gather together. Over the centuries, more emphasis has been placed on our houses of worship, but the church is still the collection of people. A church building is just the place where they meet.

And yet our places of worship have taken shape around us. That is, there are certain qualities specific to the buildings where people meet to worship, and it all has to do with how we worship. The earliest Christians met in homes. When more room was required, they rented lecture halls. When Christians built their own houses of worship, these were basically just big rooms where a lot of people could

113

meet. Over time, these rooms developed two main points of focus—the altar and the pulpit—for the two main activities of Christian worship: the Lord's Supper and the preaching of the Word. Roman Catholic churches, whose worship revolves around Communion, kept the altar most central, while Protestant churches exalted the pulpit because of their emphasis on preaching.

Synagogues are similar to Protestant churches, with an emphasis on prayer and instruction. Architecturally, they are very simple, with room where many can meet. That's what the word "synagogue" means: gathering place. And the Muslim tradition is quite the same. People gather in mosques for prayers, readings, some washing rituals, and fellowship. They are careful to offer their prayers in the direction of Mecca, their holy city.

There's an interesting distinction within these three great traditions. Even within Christianity, there are distinctions. Roman Catholic churches (and even more so the Eastern Orthodox) freely use images of saints and biblical scenes to adorn the worship space. Protestant churches tend to avoid such images, as a protest against what the early Reformers saw as idolatry. Because of the Second

Commandment, Jewish worship excludes "graven images." Muslims have a similar prohibition, although many mosques are adorned with beautiful abstract and geometric designs.

Hindu worship, both in temples and at household shrines, overflows with a celebration of beauty. Many images are present, depicting various gods and goddesses, as participants engage in ritual chanting and singing, often with incense and instruments. All the senses come into play. Buddhism has many different varieties, some more ornate than others. Public worship involves chanting and teaching, and private meditation and chanting are encouraged as well. The house of worship may include trees, water, or other natural elements.

Q: Can a non-Christian take the Lord's Supper?

A: This is really a question to ask the leaders of your church. Some denominations are very protective of the Communion experience; others are more open. When visiting in any house of worship, you want to observe the "house rules," whether you agree with them or not. If a particular church restricts the Lord's Supper to members of that church or denomination, don't fight it.

In general, however, we could say that the Lord's Supper is intended and designed for Christians. It originated with the Passover meal Jesus shared with his closest followers, and ever since it has been a commitment to unity within the church. We share this "meal" in common with other believers in remembrance of the Lord we adore. A non-Christian, by definition, does not share in that commonality.

Yet, it must be said that Jesus dined with all sorts of people—tax collectors and prostitutes as well as Pharisees. He didn't bar anyone from his table. So he probably wouldn't be too upset today if a non-Christian wanted to join in this Christian ritual.

Think about the act of taking Communion and what it symbolizes. It is a receiving of Christ and his sacrifice into ourselves. It is a vivid picture of "accepting Jesus," and maybe more than just a picture. It is an act by which Christians connect with Jesus Christ. If a non-Christian understands that meaning and still wants to participate, then . . . well, that person might not remain a non-Christian much longer.

CHAPTER SEVEN

The Bible's Uniqueness

C hristians believe the Bible is the only authoritative
*Scripture because it is God's actual Word to us.
Although God used humans to write this holy book,
Christians maintain that the Bible is inerrant and
infallible. What it says about God is unquestionably
accurate, and how it commands us to live is entirely
trustworthy. That being the case, the Bible is applicable
in all that we say, do, and think.*

Q: Who wrote the Bible?

A: The books of the Bible were written over a
span of more than a thousand years by at least
30 different authors. Some of the books—Paul's
epistles and most of the prophetic books—clearly
name their authors, while others are anonymous.
Church tradition, however, has identified the writers
of many of the anonymous works as well. The
identities of the authors of only a few books, like

the Book of Hebrews, are in doubt. Nevertheless,
the church still regards them as divinely inspired
because their content is consistent with the rest of
Scripture and because the early church regarded
these books as authoritative.

The first five books of the Bible have been called the
"Books of Moses" even though there's nothing within
them that claims Mosaic authorship. Yet, ancient
Hebrew tradition attributes these books to Moses,
and Jesus and the New Testament writers also made
that assumption.

In modern times, scholars have sifted through the
five books of Moses and tried to determine the
original sources of these documents. Some have
suggested that Ezra or another scribe created the
final edition as late as the fifth century B.C. In the
same way, scholars surmise that later sections of
Isaiah were written by a "second Isaiah" and even
a third, working in the name and tradition of the
eighth-century prophet.

These theories don't need to be a problem for the
serious student of Scripture. The fact remains that we
understand the ultimate author of biblical truth to be
God. "No prophecy ever came by human will," the

apostle Peter wrote, "but men and women moved by the Holy Spirit spoke from God" (2 Peter 1:21). The human author might be Moses or Ezra, Jeremiah or his secretary, but God inspired all of Scripture, and we can trust it to present God's truth to us.

The divine inspiration of the Bible is a tricky issue. In a few cases, such as the Ten Commandments, it seems that God directly dictated his message. But most of Scripture uses the unique skills and insights of the human authors. No doubt David's experiences as a shepherd enhanced the Twenty-Third Psalm, while Paul's lawyerlike logic graces the Book of Romans. Inspiration does not necessarily mean dictation. We embrace the mystery of Jesus being fully God and fully human. In the same way, we understand the Bible's origins to be both divine and human.

Q: How were books selected to be in the Bible?

A: The Hebrew Scriptures (what Christians call the Old Testament) were developed and cradled within the Jewish religion. Apparently the five "Books of Moses" that begin the Bible were present in some form quite early. For instance, during repair work on the Jerusalem Temple in the 620s B.C., the "Book of the Law" was discovered there (2 Kings 22:8). This tells us two things—that there was an authoritative Scripture in existence and that it had been forgotten for a while.

As for the historical books, it seems that royal scribes maintained official records, which were preserved through the generations. In fact, the Books of Kings and Chronicles tell the same history from two different perspectives. Chronicles seem to be the official records of the southern kingdom of Judah, while Kings might have come from the northern kingdom or perhaps from an independent prophet who was familiar with both nations. The historians of Scripture also "footnote" several other sources, works which have been either lost or folded into our present accounts.

Hebrew tradition credits the scribe Ezra with the major compilation of the Hebrew Scriptures. Scholars agree that he or other scribes of his time (400s B.C.) pulled together most of these documents. There were only minor disagreements on the content of the

Hebrew Bible, though various collections tweaked the order of the books.

Sometime between 250 and 100 B.C., the Hebrew Scriptures were translated into Greek, known as the *Septuagint*. The translators included additional recent Jewish works that the Jewish community respected but were not included with sacred Scripture. These books became known as the Apocrypha, meaning "hidden," because they were absent ("hidden") from the Hebrew Scriptures. As the Christian church adopted the Greek Old Testament, many included the Apocrypha with the biblical books. A millennium later, Protestants reverted to the Hebrew model and removed the Apocrypha from their Scripture while the Roman Catholic Church officially accepted these books into their canon of Scripture.

How did the New Testament books come together? Sometimes people assume that a church council decided this, but the process was much less official than that. Very early, churches were sharing the writings of the apostles and their colleagues.

At the end of his letter to the Colossians (4:16), Paul asked them to swap epistles with another church nearby. This activity probably occurred frequently, even in the first century—churches copying epistles and adding them to their collection. Remarkably, Peter mentioned the way Paul wrote "all his letters" (3:16), which further indicates that this collecting was taking place. It also compares these epistles to "the other scriptures," hinting that Paul's letters were already revered.

The four Gospels had been collected by the middle of the second century and possibly much earlier. Local churches developed their lists of accepted readings. The crucial factor in this acceptance was apostolic standing. A book had to be written by an apostle or someone very close to an apostle. (Thus, Mark's Gospel was admitted because he was writing Peter's memoirs, and Luke's Gospel was accepted because he was a companion of Paul. John and Matthew were apostles themselves, so naturally their Gospels would be readily approved.)

It was actually a heretic who spurred the church to be more cautious and intentional about naming its Scriptures. Following an anti-Jewish Gnosticism in the mid–100s, a leader named Marcion compiled a New Testament collection with only half of Luke and most of Paul's letters. Meanwhile, we have a document dating from the late 100s that seems to be the Scripture list of the church at Rome—and almost identical to our current New Testament. For another century or so, there was mild debate about certain books. Some churches excluded Jude or 2 Peter or James, while others included epistles from Barnabas or Clement. But in 367, Bishop Athanasius of Alexandria named our present 27 books as the Christian Scriptures, and this choice was confirmed at the Council of Carthage in 397.

Q: How was the Bible preserved over the centuries?

A: Scribes made copies of the sacred and historical documents of ancient Israel. Ezra was the most notable of the Old Testament scribes. Over the next few centuries, scribes became religious leaders (like Ezra), not just secretaries. Long before the invention of the modern printing press, the work of these scribes was crucial in the dissemination of Scripture.

The scribal tradition developed its own system of checks and balances to ensure that these holy words were copied accurately. Modern archaeology has given us an interesting vantage point on the accuracy of these scribes' work. For a long period, the earliest copy of the Hebrew Scriptures we had was the Masoretic Text, dating back to the A.D. 700s or thereabouts. But then the Dead Sea Scrolls were discovered, which contained significant fragments of several Old Testament books that dated back to the first century and earlier. How had the text changed in seven centuries? Hardly at all. As the monastic tradition developed within Christianity in the late 300s and beyond, the monks took on the role of scribe, carefully copying both Testaments.

In Old Testament times, documents were written on papyrus, an early form of paper made from reeds. Later scribes used parchment, also known as vellum, which was made from animal skin. In the Hebrew tradition, pages were attached in scroll form. When Jesus first spoke in his hometown synagogue, he was handed the scroll of Isaiah, which he unrolled to a particular place to read (Luke 4:17). That scroll tradition lives on in synagogues today.

Already in the first century A.D. and increasingly thereafter, parchment pages would be put together in what was called a *codex*. This was merely an early book form, with pages stacked and attached. We

have several codices of the Bible text that date back
to the A.D. 300s and 400s and numerous papyri of
Scripture fragments that date even earlier.

No, we don't have the original documents of biblical
writings, but we have a huge number of manuscripts
that were copied very early, some within a century
of the originals. There are minor differences among
these manuscripts, owing to scribal error, but far
fewer than you'd expect. And most experts say these
differences have no bearing on any major church
teaching. In all, the biblical text has been preserved
extremely well. The level of confidence in the Bible
text is far better than any other ancient writing.

Q: Does the Bible have any errors?

A: The short answer is no, but let's take a deeper
look at the issue. If we believe the Bible is the
divinely inspired word of God, then we can be
confident that it speaks the truth. God would not
deceive us, nor would he make errors.

In this process of inspiration, however, God chose to
use human authors with their own skills, experience,

and knowledge. He moved them to write his
message, but he also gave them some leeway. So
we find the biblical authors, people of their own
time, expressing God's truth in ways appropriate to
their culture. To our modern minds, some of these
expressions might seem like errors.

For instance, the Bible was written in a time when
people believed the sun revolved around the Earth.
Now we know better. So is it an error when we
read, "In the heavens he has set a tent for the
sun. . . . Its rising is from the end of the heavens,
and its circuit to the end of them" (Psalm 19:4, 6)?
No, the psalmist is not teaching a science lesson,
just using an image understood by the people
of his day.

Some have pointed out discrepancies in parallel
passages in the Gospels and some Old Testament
history. Did 100,000 or 130,000 go to battle? Certainly
we can let one of the historians round off a number.
And we must not apply the demands of modern
journalism to the Gospel accounts. In an era when
history was passed on orally from generation to
generation, paraphrasing was quite acceptable.

The Bible is not a scientific treatise, though it says many true things about the world God created. It teaches us the truth about God and humanity—and we can trust its testimony while understanding that God used time-bound humans to write it.

Q: How do I know that the stories of the Bible are reliable and trustworthy?

A: There are three ways. First, how does your own life confirm the Bible's teaching? Most Christians would say that the Bible describes the human condition and the goodness of God in a remarkably accurate way. People who read the Bible for the first time are often dazzled because they find themselves in those pages. That is, the teachings of Scripture match up with their own experience. And so, with this personal corroboration of the truth of scriptural teaching, it's perfectly reasonable to believe that its stories are true as well.

Second, there has been a convincing amount of historical research verifying the stories of Scripture. In fact, there have been several examples in the last

century or so of skeptics who set out to disprove
Christianity, but they ended up converting to the
Christian faith. No, we don't have corroborating
archaeological evidence for everything in Scripture,
but there are more and more finds that support the
biblical account.

Here's one case. In the verse of the Christmas
story that everyone skips over, Luke mentions that
Quirinius was governor of Syria when Jesus was
born. For quite a while, scholars took issue with
this. They had records of Quirinius as the Syrian
governor, but several years *after* Jesus was born.
Luke must have goofed on this one, they claimed.
But then an inscription was found, listing the
governors of Syria. Quirinius had two terms, the
later one everyone knew about and an *early* one
that would correspond with the time of Jesus' birth.
And that isn't the only time this sort of thing has
happened. The more we learn of the archaeology of
the biblical period, the more corroboration we get.

The third point is merely a matter of logic. We
believe in a supernatural God who cares about
the people he has created. He cares enough to
communicate with us. The stories of Scripture are
part of this communication. Skeptics wonder how

a man can walk on water or how water can turn to wine. Could the Red Sea really part? Could a boy kill a giant? Could a man survive in a den of lions?

Well, why not? This is the Creator of the universe were talking about. He made the sea—do you think it would be that tough for him to split it apart? C. S. Lewis claimed that people are either naturalists or supernaturalists. Naturalists see the world as a closed system. Miracles strain belief. But, as people touched by God, we Christians are miracles ourselves. So we have no trouble believing that God has done amazing, supernatural things in history.

Q: I like reading the New Testament. What does the Old Testament have to offer?

A: The Old Testament has a wealth of godly wisdom and is well worth reading. Let's consider five of the many benefits when studying this section of Scripture.

1. Good and bad examples. Discussing the experiences of Old Testament Israel, the apostle Paul wrote, "These things happened to them to serve as an example, and they were written down to instruct us" (1 Corinthians 10:11). In many passages of the Hebrew Scriptures, we find stories of faith and folly, wisdom and wantonness. Abraham and Sarah trusted God, Jacob wrestled with him, and Moses took a chance on doing God's will. Ruth showed loyalty, David showed passion in good and bad pursuits alike, and Elijah crowed in victory and moped in depression. Using the prophet as an example of effective prayer, James says, "Elijah was a human being like us" (James 5:17). They all were. And we can learn much from all of them.

2. How God works. Of course, the starring role of the Old Testament belongs not to Abraham, Sarah, Ruth, or David, but to God. He is the active agent who delivers his people and woos them. Studying these stories, we see how God uses the weak to confound the strong, how he operates in his own timing even when people begin to doubt him, how he prefers obedience to ritual sacrifice, and how he answers prayer.

3. What God requires. God gave "the Law" (Torah) to Israel with its assortment of moral, ceremonial, governmental, and health regulations. Now the New Testament makes it clear that Christians are not bound by the Law. We are free in Christ, living in the grace of God. That changes our relationship with Old Testament laws, but it doesn't erase it. We should still care deeply about the kind of behavior God required of his people in that time. And in our continuing desire to please God in our own culture, we can sift through his ancient commands to learn his will for us today. We can also read the words of the prophets, as they applied God's laws to changing situations, always calling their people (and us) to humble obedience, authentic service, and a growing relationship with the Lord.

4. The heart of God. "I have loved you with an everlasting love," God told his people through the prophet Jeremiah (Jeremiah 31:3). The psalmist writes, "As a father has compassion for his children, so the Lord has compassion for those who fear him" (Psalm 103:13). Again and again, we read God's emotional outpouring. He is a caring parent, a jilted lover, a loyal friend, and a diligent shepherd. If God ever seems cold and distant to you, read the psalms and the prophets to get a glimpse of his heart.

5. The background of Christ. As you know, Jesus was Jewish and lived in Palestine. He worshipped at the Temple in Jerusalem, studied at the local synagogue, and observed Jewish holy days. A rabbi who often quoted the Hebrew Scriptures, Jesus called himself the Son of Man (alluding to the Book of Daniel). There are many other correlations. The Last Supper, for example, was a Passover meal. More importantly, Jesus fulfilled many Old Testament prophecies, which indicate that Jesus is the promised Messiah. Indeed, how can you fully understand Jesus' sacrificial death without knowing about Old Testament sacrifices? If you want to understand Jesus, you need to know the world into which he came. The Hebrew Scriptures will open a window onto that world.

Q: Is the God of the Old Testament a God of wrath and the God of the New Testament a God of love?

A: Many people have glanced at the Old and New Testaments and assumed something like that, but the closer you examine the Bible, the more you sense a consistency between the two testaments' view of God. The Old Testament actually portrays God in a

far more loving way than some people think, and
the New Testament might also surprise them with
the harshness of some of its teachings.

Do the Old Testament laws seem rigid and unfeeling
with brutal punishment for minor offenses? If so,
take a look at Deuteronomy, where you are called
to "love the Lord your God with all your heart,
and with all your soul, and with all your might"
(Deuteronomy 6:5). The law is set within a context
of love. When you view it in this way, you can see
that many of the seemingly picky health regulations
were actually amazingly modern ways to keep the
people disease free. Commands like "an eye for an
eye" were actually protective in an age when you
could get killed for accidentally knocking out a
guy's tooth. And while the Law included capital
punishment, it also provided a kind of appeal
system in the form of "cities of refuge" to where
those guilty of manslaughter could flee to receive
a fair trial.

Maybe the prophets seem too shrill for us, always
scolding the people for their sins. But read Hosea,
where God shows himself as a heartsick husband.
In many prophetic passages, God admits that he's
deeply in love with Israel, and he longs for them

to love him back. Moreover, God commanded his people to treat the poor fairly, to provide for widows and orphans, and to do good toward strangers.

But then there are the times when God orders his people to go to war against other nations—and not just to fight them but to exterminate them. These Old Testament passages are certainly bothersome material. The loving God of Deuteronomy and Hosea suddenly seems like a monster.

There's no easy answer for those problem passages. Some say these commands arise from overzealous Israelite warriors *assuming* God was just as zealous as they were, but that raises more problems than it solves. We must remember that God often admitted he was jealous, and he didn't want to share his people's love with any of the false gods worshipped by Israel's neighbors. The surrounding nations weren't just political entities; they were religious cultures. The Israelites' neighbors, the Canaanites, for example, practiced a sex-based fertility religion that sacrificed their children. God did not want the Canaanites and other peoples like them to seduce his people, which did occur on many occasions.

Some folks think that the New Testament is all about how nice God is. It surprises them to read some of Jesus' teachings about God's judgment. Jesus often mentioned hell and warned about the harsh consequences of unbelief. It's sweet to read how he identifies with the "least of these my brothers" and commends those who treated the needy with kindness. But we often gloss over the part where he condemns others to the lake of fire for failing to show kindness to needy people.

The whole truth is that God is both righteous and loving. Awesome in his holiness, he must pass judgment on sin. Meanwhile, his amazing love reaches out for a genuine relationship with us. These two qualities met at the cross, where he punished the sins of the world by taking them on himself.

Q: Every religion seems to have its own scriptures. How do I know that the Bible is true and unique?

A: There might be many biographies written about a public figure, but when that person puts out an autobiography, that's a publishing event! Why? Because the celebrity is now telling his or her own story. We're getting the inside scoop, not just conjecture from outside observers.

As Christians see it, that's the main difference between the Bible and the scriptures of other religions. Certainly there have been many wise sages who have written insightful things about God, but we believe the Bible is God's own story. In these pages he shares himself with us.

Don't, however, get into a shouting match with people of other faiths: "Our holy book is better than yours!" "No, it's not!" That's a pointless exercise, especially since *our* holy book requires that we act with humility and love. Moreover, the Bible can speak for itself. "Indeed, the word of God is living and active," Paul wrote, "sharper than any two-edged sword, piercing until it divides soul from spirit, joints from marrow; it is able to judge the thoughts and intentions of the heart" (Hebrews 4:12). If people read the Bible with an open heart, we can trust God to get through to them.

The factor that makes the Bible truly unique is that it is the book about Jesus, the unique Son of God,

our Lord and Savior. The Hebrew Scripture presents
the problem of sin, portrays the process of ritual
sacrifice, and prophesies about a deliverer to come.
The New Testament tells the story of Jesus, who
became our sacrifice for sin, and it explains how we
can know our heavenly Father through him. This is
what the Bible has that no other religious scripture
can tell us.

Q: Why do people refer to the Bible as "the
Holy Bible"? How is it different? Inspired?

A: Do you know that the word *Bible* means
"book"? It comes from the Latin *biblia*. Even today,
in Latin-based languages, the Bible is simply "the
book." In medieval times, that was literally true in
many communities throughout Europe. There would
be one book in town, the Bible, which was kept
in the church. As more books were written and
distributed, especially after the invention of the
printing press, it became important to designate the
Bible as *sacra biblia*—not just any book, but the
holy book, God's book.

When the King James Version of the Bible was first published in 1611, its title page used this designation: Holy Bible. This became the dominant English version for several centuries, so virtually all Bibles had that title stamped on their covers.

It's an appropriate term since Christians hold that the Bible is inspired by God (the word *inspired* means "God-breathed"). It is the book by God and about God, and it leads us to God. And yet, in English the term "Holy Bible" is a bit redundant. Any Bible is holy, whether it has those words stamped on the cover or not.

Some publishers have experimented with just printing "Bible" on the cover, but then some people think it's a different book, something less holy than a "Holy Bible." No need to worry. There is no difference between a "Bible" and a "Holy Bible." That's just a matter of titling. They are the same where it counts—on the inside.

Q: There seems to be so many translations of the Bible—how do I choose one? And why isn't there just one translation?

A: Language—any language—is rooted in its home culture. Translating from one language to another is a cultural exchange, not just a matter of consulting a dictionary and plugging in words. There are tribes in tropical areas that have no word for snow. (Why would they need one?) How would you translate a *Times* article for them about a blizzard paralyzing New York?

In any tongue, words have nuances and double meanings. "The fire chief was so fired up after the fire that he fired all the firefighters." Try explaining that to someone who didn't grow up speaking English.

The same thing is true when we try to translate the language of ancient Israel into modern English. The words used by David, Solomon, Elijah, and Isaiah have shades of meaning that are difficult to capture in English. *Shalom* means peace, but also contentment, prosperity, hello, goodbye, and "How ya doin'?"

The way we speak also changes through time. Twenty years ago, if you had said you were "surfing the net," you'd get a lot of blank stares. And we don't just have new words; we have new rhythms. Watch some sitcom reruns from the fifties, and listen to the language. You can understand it, sure, but it sounds a bit old-fashioned.

For more than three centuries, English-speaking Christians used the King James Version (sometimes known as the Authorized Version), which was translated in 1611. This was an amazing work for its time, and it has helped shape the English language. But in the mid–1900s, some wanted a fresher translation. The Revised Standard Version began to break the KJV monopoly, and later the New International Version and others found acceptance. The internal differences among these new translations were minimal; they just had different markets. The RSV took hold in mainline Protestant denominations, while the NIV was developed for evangelicals. The more literal New American Standard Bible (and later the New King James Version) appealed to fundamentalists. The Living Bible, admittedly a free paraphrase of the scriptural text, caught the wave of the Jesus Movement and gained great popularity among youth.

The last two decades have seen an explosion of new Bible versions. Some are revisions of standard translations for adult readers who want an accurate, yet easily understood translation. Other paraphrased versions are aimed for younger readers.

How can you choose a version to use? Well, first you can relax because all of these are fairly accurate translations. None of them will lead you astray. Then you should consider what your church uses. If you want to follow along with the preaching or teaching, it would help to be on the same page, literally. But then you want to find a Bible that speaks your language. Is it readable? Does it make sense to you?

Some people choose two Bibles—one for study and another for casual reading. In this case, you should be aware that some versions are more literal than others. That is, some provide more of a word-by-word rendering of the original languages, rather than a thought-by-thought paraphrase. The New American Standard Bible is the most literal, with New International Version, New Revised Standard Version, New King James Version, and New Jerusalem Bible also sticking rather close to the original text. Freer paraphrases include the Living Bible, the Message, and Today's English Version (aka Good News). If you're trying to read through the whole Bible in a year, grab one of these paraphrases. If you're studying a few verses at a time, the more literal versions are probably better.

Q: What is the main message of the Bible?

A: Of course, there are many important messages in the Bible: who God is; who Jesus is; how God wants us to live; and so on. But it might be better to think of the Bible as a story, a love story.

How many Hollywood stories have followed this basic formula? Boy meets girl, boy loses girl, boy gets girl back. The Bible has a similar outline, except the starring roles belong to God and humanity.

"Very good!" God exclaimed after creating the first human couple, whom he made in his image. They walked with him in the idyllic Garden of Eden. But then Adam and Eve did the very thing God asked them not to do. Consumed with guilt and shame, they couldn't look him in the eye, so they hid from him. God called and called until they finally had to face the music.

Centuries passed, and the world filled up with the human race. God chose one family to whom he would show his special love and from whom he would demand a special kind of behavior. He gave the Law to the Israelites, and he worked mightily in their history.

The Old Testament is the account of this relationship between God and his people—his laws, their history, his emotions, and their thoughts. Along the way, some individuals trusted God and enjoyed a great relationship with him. But many got sidetracked by greed, pride, or lust. The tragedy of Adam and Eve played out again and again and again, as people did the very things God asked them not to do and then hid from him in shame. Sin brought disaster on the nation, but the worst disaster was when people wandered away from God.

The Lord sent many messages to his beloved, imploring them to return to him. He kept promising them a way out of their mess. He would come to them in a new way. He would overcome the obstacles between them. He would find a solution to the sin problem, forgiving them and placing love in their hearts. In many cases, the prophets who brought these messages were persecuted or ignored.

The New Testament dawns with a miraculous birth.
There is a man who is more than a man. He teaches,
heals, and expresses the love of God for his people.
Is this just another messenger or could this be the
Lord himself, stepping into our world to demonstrate
his devotion to us? Some respond to his message
and follow him, but others conspire against him. He
eventually dies a criminal's death.

This is the moment in the movie when all seems lost.
The hero has failed in his attempt to woo those he
loves. He has given his life for his beloved, yet no
one seems to care. But then the sun rises on Easter
Sunday, and the tomb is empty. There are sightings
here and there, and finally it's verified. The Lord has
returned to life. He has prevailed over the power of
death, and now his beloved ones are free to live
forever with him.

The rest of the New Testament sorts it out,
explaining what exactly went on in those climactic
scenes. He took our sins with him into the grave,
and he raises us with him into a new life. We
hold that promise even as we continue our daily
struggles, and we look forward to a new heaven and
new earth, where we will reign with him forever.

CHAPTER EIGHT

Science, Society, and the Bible

*W*hen science and the Bible intersect in our society, the news media seem to be interested only when sparks fly. What we don't hear is how the two can nicely complement each other, especially when science confirms biblical data and when religious faith affirms scientific pursuit. Although their approach to understanding the world is different, we do not need to choose one over the other. It is really a cultural myth that science and the Christian faith are at war.

Q: Do science and the Bible conflict?

A: For the past century, science and the Bible have appeared to be at bitter odds, each claiming to hold the key to the creation of the universe. Many modern scientists deny that an intelligent being designed the world as we know it. The Bible, on the other hand, clearly attributes the formation of all things to a Supreme Being. This contention seems to be the major battle between some prominent scientists and many defenders of the Bible.

Nevertheless, the conflict really isn't between science and the Bible, for there are many respected scientists who are devout Jews and Christians. The conflict is between people who hold different world views. Actually, an alliance between science and religion existed in Western civilization between the 1500s and the late 1800s, and many of the notable scientists, such as Kepler, Boyle, Maxwell, Faraday, and Kelvin, held strong Christian convictions. Since then, society in general has become more secular, which is evident in modern science as well. Today, however, many academic societies are sponsoring conferences to promote dialogue between science and religion.

The search for truth need not divide the scientist and the person of faith. On the one hand, the Bible tells the story of why God breathed life into the first man and woman and what he expected from them; and, on the other hand, science explains how various forms of life have evolved and survived. In other words, science and the Bible simply hold different pieces to the same puzzle.

Q: Can a modern person believe in the miracles of the Bible?

A: Many of the world's leading philosophers, inventors, and great thinkers believed in the miracles of the Bible and in the awesome power of God. They saw God's presence in everything from the mysterious subatomic particles to the massive oceanic mountain ranges. Behind each miraculous event was a powerful intelligence turning the wheels of destiny and overseeing the master blueprint of creation.

As modern Christians, we see miracles all around us, and we experience them each day. A child being born into the world is a miracle. So, too, is a field of wildflowers growing in the middle of a city park. Love is a miracle. So are mercy, grace, and forgiveness, and we see those each and every day of our lives. But miracles also occur in places we never think of. The fact that the sun, moon, earth, and planets move as they do in the sky is a miracle. The laws that govern gravity and relativity are miracles to be sure. Even the incredible intricacies of the human body, such as the human eye, are miracles.

The miracles of the Bible may have happened thousands of years ago, but that doesn't mean they haven't occurred since and aren't occurring today. As you read this, somebody somewhere may be experiencing a miracle similar to one described in the Bible. Can we say with absolute certainty from our limited human perspective that the Lord of the universe cannot perform a miracle? In fact, it is no less preposterous to answer yes today than it was two thousand years ago.

And let us not forget that life itself is a miracle, and each day we are given a new chance to come to that realization.

Q: Is it true that intelligent people often reject religious faith? Is it because faith and knowledge are opposites?

A: There are many intelligent people who have no faith in God, but there are many "dumb" people who think religious faith is nonsense as well. Moreover, in a lot of cases the reason these intelligent people decide not to believe in God has far more to do with factors other than their intellectual abilities.

For example, an intelligent person may be a math professor who feels she has no time for religion. Or an intelligent person may be a rocket scientist who blames God for the untimely death of his spouse. In either case, they may have a colleague who has a deep faith in Christ.

We also know people who consider everything with only their heads and never pay the slightest bit of attention to their hearts. They are pretty smart folks, but they have little faith, if any, in anything they can't perceive with their five senses. They value only those things they can apply reason or logic to, and they think religious people have abandoned the critical faculties of their minds.

Christians, however, are not mindless zombies; certainly, God does not want us to be. "Always be ready," said Peter, "to make your defense to anyone who demands from you an accounting for the hope that is in you" (1 Peter 3:15). In other words, you should be able to intelligently explain why you believe in Jesus, which proves that the Bible does not teach that having faith excludes clear thinking.

Q: Where do dinosaurs fit in with the story of creation?

A: It is difficult to argue that dinosaurs never existed when countless dinosaur fossils are on display in scores of museums around the world. The presence of so many dinosaur fossils, however, need not undermine our faith in God and his Word. God is still the Creator, and dinosaurs were created beings. It's quite possible that dinosaurs were among the creatures listed in the Creation account in Genesis 1.

Does the word "day" in Genesis 1 refer to a 24-hour period or to an era? Did Adam and Eve name the dinosaurs, or did the dinosaurs predate humankind? Did God create the dinosaurs as already specialized creatures, or did they evolve from other life forms? Did the flood Noah survived obliterate all the dinosaurs, or did another cataclysmic disaster do them in? Does anyone really know the answers to these questions? What these questions do imply is that it is possible to reconcile the existence of dinosaurs with the biblical account of creation.

What we know today about dinosaurs based strictly on scientific research has toppled numerous notions that we had about them even a generation ago. So who is to say the notions we have about them today will not be swept away by further discoveries and advanced technology a generation from now? Of course, that leaves us on a slippery slope when we make any claims about an entire race of animals that disappeared eons ago. Nevertheless, we can't ignore the fossils they left behind, but neither can we make assertions about how dinosaurs came into being when we have no scientific record of their origins.

Dinosaurs are fascinating creatures that at one time possibly terrified our ancestors, but we should not be afraid that our children will lose their faith in God over them.

Q: How can science and the Bible complement each other?

A: Albert Einstein made an interesting comment when he said, "Science without religion is lame, religion without science is blind."

Basically, science and religion are two ways of looking at the mysterious wonders of the world while trying to explain those wonders. Science takes an empirical approach from a human perspective while religion relies on God's explanation through Scriptures. When both are working together, they can offer a powerful statement about the world we live in and how we fit into this world.

Nevertheless, the Christian faith still makes claims that science cannot support. For example, can science prove that Jesus is the Son of God and that he died for our sins? These truths are central to our beliefs as Christians; yet, if science has anything to say about them, it would be to deny their reality. The writer of Hebrews made this clear, saying, "Faith is the assurance of things hoped for, the conviction of things not seen" (Hebrews 11:1). Science has to see before it can affirm.

Thus, science can be a useful ally, but it should never be considered as part of the team. In other words, the Christian faith without science is not necessarily blind. We just place our trust in what God has said to us through Scripture.

Q: Is there any evidence of God that scholars have seen in the natural world?

A: The natural world is filled with laws and functions that point to intelligent design. There is the theory of entanglement, which states that two particles that have been in contact will continue to affect each other over massive distances. Then there's the Fibonacci Sequence, a series of numbers that appear in mathematical and geometrical measurements in so many parts of the physical world they could not possibly have been a random occurrence. So too are the many breathtaking mathematical equations that seem to govern every aspect of the universe, from pi to phi to the Golden Ratio to the Just Six Numbers theory. Something had to think that all up as they are too specific, detailed, and intricate to have happened just on a fluke!

The fact that the gigantic solar system and the tiny human eye operate with such precision is further indication that a powerful intelligence designed the natural world. It is important to say Paul's words once more: "For what can be known about God is plain to them, because God has shown it to them. Ever since the creation of the world his eternal power and divine nature, invisible though they are, have been understood and seen through the things he has made" (Romans 1:19–20).

Q: Why does our government forbid teaching religion in public schools?

A: Our nation's founders realized that religious thought was diverse and that mandating a particular religion in public schools was impossible. That's why our government forbids teaching religion in public schools. It is more to protect our religious freedoms than to take any away. After all, how could the government possibly decide which religions to teach? There are not enough hours in a school day to teach them all. There aren't even enough hours in one day to teach the many diverse forms of Christianity that exist!

In order to fully protect every person's right to worship in the way they prefer, the government has done the right thing by leaving religion out of the public schools. Imagine the fights that might break out between students who believe their religion to be the only "right" one. Look at the wars we have today, and you can see proof of what happens when one religion tries to predominate.

As an alternative, private schools can include religious instructions to supplement the curriculum. Christian parents can send their children to one of these private schools, or they can homeschool their children. Meanwhile, public schools are for basic education, and religious studies are best left to their parents to initiate after school when students are free to participate in a religious activity of their choosing.

Q: Have scientists tested the power of prayer? If so, what were the results of these studies?

A: Over the last 50 years, dozens of scientific studies, mainly in the medical community, have tried to determine the healing effects of prayer. The results of some of those studies have been inconclusive, but many indicate a direct relationship between prayer and increased levels of well-being among seriously ill patients, even when the patients did not know they were being prayed for.

ABC News recently reported on a major study that took place at Duke University Medical Center, in which prayers were directed at cardiology patients, many of whom noted beneficial results. Another fascinating study covered by ABC News and available on their Web site occurred at Mid America Heart Institute in Kansas City, Missouri. This study also involved cardiology patients, and a skeptical doctor named James O'Keefe was openly amazed at the positive results.

Dr. Elizabeth Targ also conducted the AIDS prayer studies at the Pacific College of Medicine, which examined 20 patients, 10 of whom were prayed over in addition to regular medical services. Of the 20, the 10 who received prayer showed six times fewer and shorter hospitalizations than those who did not receive prayer.

Another well-publicized test involved 100 heart patients at San Francisco General Hospital. Half were given high-tech medical treatment while the other half received treatment and prayer. None of the patients knew if they were in the prayer group or not, but the half who did receive prayer did far better than those who did not. The prayed-for group showed faster healing and recovery rates.

Just a quick search on the Internet turns up many of these prayer research studies. More and more medical professionals are using prayer or are studying the possible effects on their patients. It seems that the medical and scientific communities are becoming much more open-minded about the power of prayer.

Q: As a Christian I believe God heals. But does this mean I should not go to my doctor? Doesn't a visit to the doctor show a lack of faith?

A: God heals, and, as Jesus taught us, we do have the power to heal others and ourselves through faith in Jesus Christ. But that does not restrict Christians from turning to those whom God has gifted with specialized medical skills. Indeed, many doctors are devoted Christians, and, lest we forget, Luke, the author of one of the Gospels and a faithful companion of Paul, was a physician who often nursed Paul's wounds.

Since God gives each of us special gifts, and since God chooses to express his power through people in different ways, no Christian should ever feel guilty about visiting a doctor. After all, who gave that doctor the ability to understand the human body and heal? God. Just as God gives some of us the gift of writing and others the gift of hospitality, he also gives doctors and nurses a special talent at helping others to heal. Think of doctors and their staffs as angels in lab coats!

All believers have the divine power within to heal any ills that befall them. Most of us, however, don't have that complete, unquestionable faith that Jesus saw in the woman whose faith made her whole when she touched his cloak in a crowd. Nor do we have the faith of the two blind men who were given sight when Jesus touched their eyes and said, "According to your faith let it be done to you" (Matthew 9:29). But we shouldn't feel bad; we are in good company. Even Jesus' own disciples often had less-than-perfect faith!

CHAPTER NINE

Tell Me About Heaven and Hell

*M*ost people, and young people in particular, are so busy that they give little thought about what will happen to them after they die. In those quiet moments, however, when we have lost a loved one or when a serious illness afflicts us, we can't help but wonder about the afterlife. The Bible provides glimpses of heaven and hell, and they can give us either inner peace or unsettling dread.

Q: What will happen the moment I die?

A: While the apostle Paul sensed his death approaching, he mused about the possibilities. It was clearly a win-win situation. "For to me, living is Christ and dying is gain," he wrote to the Christians in Philippi (Philippians 1:21). He also said staying alive and helping others would be good, but "my desire is to depart and be with Christ, for that is far better" (Philippians 1:23). Elsewhere, he said, "We would rather be away from the body and at home with the Lord" (2 Corinthians 5:8).

It's clear that Paul understood physical death for the Christian as an immediate transition into the presence of the Lord. This is confirmed by Jesus' comment to the thief crucified beside him: "Today you will be with me in Paradise" (Luke 23:43).

Other biblical teachings look forward to Christ's triumphant return at the end of time. Those who have died "in Christ" will be given imperishable bodies (1 Corinthians 15:52), perhaps like the body Jesus had after his resurrection. We will then reign with Jesus over a new heaven and a new earth (2 Timothy 2:12; Revelation 20:6).

But what happens in the meantime between our death and Christ's return? Well, remember that we cross from time into eternity. "With the Lord one day is like a thousand years, and a thousand years are like one day" (2 Peter 3:8). All we know from Scripture is that those of us who trust him will be "with the Lord" for this timeless period.

Q: Should I take seriously those "near-death" experiences in which people temporarily die and claim to have seen the world to come?

A: Yes, we can take them seriously, but we don't need to take them authoritatively. The truth is, we don't know all the details of what happens after death. It's quite interesting that many who "die" temporarily report the same sort of sensations—floating above their own bodies, moving through a long tunnel toward a bright light, and seeing loved ones along the way. But is this heaven? Is this a spiritual experience at all? We can't say for sure.

Some Christians have suggested that near-death experiences are cases of demonic deception, but it's not necessary to go that far. The sensations might be merely physical processes of the brain, which people interpret in these common spiritual ways.

Then again, maybe there is a spiritual reality here. Maybe this passageway toward the light is just the entry path to more biblical experiences. We must remain humble as we evaluate matters of life after death because honestly there's a lot the Bible doesn't tell us. Nevertheless, we shouldn't build our theology on these near-death experiences, no matter how intriguing they may appear. It's better to stick with what the Bible tells us and keep an open mind about the rest.

Q: Who will be in heaven?

A: The New Testament unequivocally says those who trust in Jesus will enjoy eternity with God in heaven. In one of the best-known verses of the Bible, Jesus said, "For God so loved the world that he gave his only Son, *so that everyone who believes in him may not perish but may have eternal life"* (John 3:16, italics added). That's confirmed later in the same chapter—"Whoever believes in the Son has eternal life" (John 3:36)—and in many other Scriptures. Everyone who has decided to follow Jesus will be in heaven.

We also assume that people of faith from the Old Testament will join us in heaven. Abraham's faith was counted as righteousness (Genesis 15:6; Romans 4:3), and there were certainly many others who trusted in God's goodness. Even though Jesus had not arrived yet, we can guess that God applied the *future* sacrifice of Christ Jesus to cover the sins of those people.

And that opens the door to some other possibilities. Will God forgive faithful people through the blood of Christ even if they've never heard of Christ? Because Scripture isn't clear on that matter, we should be careful what conclusions we draw. We do know that Jesus is the only way to the heavenly Father (John 14:6). We also know that God's love is overwhelming (Romans 8:38–39).

There's another sense we get from the teaching of Jesus. He spoke often about the kingdom of God, telling many parables. One consistent factor in those stories is *surprise*. People are surprised about who gets into God's kingdom. Whether it's the folks who come to the banquet from the highways and byways (see Luke 14:23), or the grape-pickers who only worked one hour (see Matthew 20:12), or the prostitutes and tax collectors who got in ahead of the Pharisees (see Matthew 21:31), the citizens of God's kingdom may include some people you least expect.

Q: Will I meet Jesus in heaven?
Will I recognize people in heaven?

A: Yes, we will meet Jesus. That's what heaven is all about, being in the presence of God the Father, Son, and Holy Spirit. And Jesus made that precise promise to the thief on the cross: He will be with Jesus in paradise.

As for recognizing others, we have a few scriptural hints that we will know one another—and Jesus—at a much deeper level. Toward the end of his famous "Love Chapter" (1 Corinthians 13), Paul talked about love as an eternal thing. We understand love at this deeper level only partially as we wait for God to bring matters to completion. "For now we see in a mirror, dimly, but then we will see face to face. Now I know only in part; then I will know fully, even as I have been fully known" (1 Corinthians 13:12). Certainly Paul was talking about our relationship with the Lord, but within this chapter on human love, he might also have been talking about our relationships with one another.

John did some similar musing in his first epistle. "Beloved, we are God's children now; what we will be has not yet been revealed. What we do know is this: when he [Jesus] is revealed, we will be like him, for we will see him as he is" (1 John 3:2). Thus, we will finally see Jesus in all his fullness in heaven. Then we will be like him.

Q: Will heaven be interesting or boring? Please explain what we'll do there.

A: Somehow people got the idea that our heavenly existence will involve sitting on clouds and playing harps. Imagine doing that eternally. Lots of comedians have quipped that they'd rather go to the other place because the people there obviously know how to have a good time.

Seriously, the symbols in the Book of Revelation culminate in something we all understand quite well: a wedding reception. "Blessed are those who are invited to the marriage supper of the Lamb," said the angel, who essentially asked John to send out invitations (Revelation 19:9). The Lamb of God is Jesus, and in this heavenly moment he finally takes a bride—the church, that is, the people who have dedicated their lives to him.

Later in this book, we get a description of eternal life with God. "The home of God is among mortals. He will dwell with them; they will be his peoples, and God himself will be with them; he will wipe every tear from their eyes. Death will be no more; mourning and crying and pain will be no more," God said. "I am making all things new" (Revelation 21:3–5). We're not talking "same old, same old" here. We will be with the Creator of the universe. Everything is new and different. In that context, we could probably add, "Boredom will be no more."

What will we be doing? Scripture doesn't give us many specifics. The details of that dimension are probably beyond our current understanding. But the key factor is we'll be with God, and we know he is the source of joy, humor, and love. No doubt our heavenly lives will overflow with these qualities.

Q: Will people in hell be aware of their errors and their consequences? Is this cruel?

A: The Bible doesn't say a lot about the afterlife. We get just a few glimpses of heaven and even less of hell. The best snapshot comes in a parable Jesus told about a rich man and a poor beggar named Lazarus (Luke 16:19–31). In this story the rich man ends up in hell (literally "Hades") and sees Lazarus enjoying heavenly luxury. The rich man complains of his "agony" in the "flames" and begs for a drop of cool water. He is reminded that things had been just the opposite during his lifetime.

Keep in mind that this is a parable, so perhaps it's less of a snapshot and more of an impressionist painting. Jesus was not trying to teach about the precise nature of heaven and hell, but he was using common imagery to express the turnabout the afterlife would bring. And yet, the Bible often speaks of hell as a "lake of fire," and Jesus frequently referred to the "weeping and gnashing of teeth" that would occur in eternal punishment.

So even though the evidence is scanty, it does lead us to surmise that, yes, people in hell will be aware of their situation and what got them there. Is that cruel? Maybe. But it's hell! They're being punished! That's the whole point.

Yet, C. S. Lewis and others have offered an intriguing suggestion. Perhaps hell is a continuing choice people make. That is, if heaven is being with God, hell is being without him, and these people who have rejected God during their lifetimes continue to reject him after death. The bus is ready to drive them heavenward, but for one reason or another they refuse to enter heaven. Instead, they consign themselves to the torment of an eternity without God and those who love God.

That's an interesting thought, and there might be a way it can fit with Scripture, but we just can't say for certain. All we really know is that hell is a place of eternal judgment, which we can avoid by trusting in God's grace.

Q: Do Christians believe in reincarnation?

A: Reincarnation is a fundamental concept of Hinduism, which teaches that souls transmigrate into other living beings, and not necessarily into human bodies, after death and at the conception of those other beings. In recent years, Western civilization has dabbled with ideas of reincarnation, and some people have sought to learn about their supposed "past lives."

The Bible does not teach reincarnation. In fact, we read, "It is appointed for mortals to die once, and after that the judgment" (Hebrews 9:27). The context of that verse points out a big difference between Christian teachings and the Hindu-based ideas of reincarnation. The Lord God has a plan. Jesus as the Israelite high priest "has appeared once for all at the end of the age to remove sin by the sacrifice of himself" (Hebrews 9:26). His single sacrifice paid for our sin, and he's coming back not to offer another sacrifice but to welcome those "who are eagerly waiting for him" (Hebrews 9:28). Thus, the Judeo-Christian view of time is linear.

Reincarnation, meanwhile, is cyclical. Life goes on and on in an endless circle. Souls, as well as human history, are recycled again and again. In the Christian view, life moves forward to a particular goal. There's a beginning, a middle, and a glorious eternity ahead—not just for our own lives but for the whole created order.

Yet, there are those who claim that reincarnation is consistent with biblical teachings. After all, didn't Jesus say John the Baptist was Elijah (Matthew 11:14)? What Jesus meant is that John was fulfilling the prophesied *role* of Elijah and not that John was the reincarnation of Elijah. Moreover, no other Scripture even comes close to supporting that concept.

Q: How are my sins forgiven today?

A: When you place your faith in Jesus and believe he has saved you, God puts all your sins on Jesus' account. And remember Jesus has already paid the death penalty for your sins. You are forgiven through the sacrificial blood of Christ.

The Bible speaks about this forgiveness in many ways, using terms such as *saved, redeemed,* and *justified,* but the story is consistent: You cannot earn your own forgiveness by being good; you must trust in *God's* goodness to forgive you through the blood of Jesus (Ephesians 2:8–9; Romans 5:8).

What *do* we have to do then? Once again, the Bible uses many terms for the same thing. We *repent,* expressing our sorrow for our sins (Acts 2:38). We *confess* our sins (1 John 1:9). We *believe in* Jesus, putting our faith in him (Acts 16:31). We *call on* the name of the Lord (Romans 10:13). We *receive* Jesus

(John 1:12). That's not a list of requirements. Those are many facets of a single heart-and-life response. In any and all of these ways, we *claim* the forgiveness that God offers.

Imagine a teenager getting arrested for public drunkenness. Unable to pay the hefty fine, the youth is thrown into the local jail. But one day the warden unlocks the prison door and says, "There's someone out there who just paid your fine. He says he's your father. He knows you haven't talked to him for a while, but he wants to make things right. He's waiting there for you, and the fine is paid, so you're free to go." What does that kid have to do now? Claim the gift. Walk out of the prison and into a new relationship with his father. That's the response we need to make when confronted with the saving work of Christ on our behalf.

But what happens if we keep sinning? It's all well and good to say our past sins are wiped away, but what about future sins? And what about those sinful habits we just can't kick?

The principle of grace still applies. We cannot earn God's forgiveness; it is a gift we must receive with gratitude. The blood of Christ is still on our account, paying for our sins even before we commit them. "If we confess our sins," John said, "he who is faithful and just will forgive us our sins and cleanse us from all unrighteousness" (1 John 1:9). That "confession" is not necessarily a visit to a priest or pastor (though that's not a bad idea). We can make that confession directly to God. The Lord's Prayer includes a simple prayer of confession that we can offer up any time we need to. "Forgive us our debts, as we also have forgiven our debtors" (Matthew 6:12).

That raises another question. If we hold grudges against others, do we forfeit our own forgiveness? A couple of verses in Scripture seem to say so, but that would make our salvation dependent on our own moral behavior, which it clearly isn't. When we receive God's forgiveness, we step into a world of grace in which we understand that all humans make mistakes. Our salvation is not some badge that allows us to judge others. On the contrary, it is a heart-softener that makes us aware of people's common need for a Savior. The word for "confess" in biblical Greek is literally to "say the same thing." When we confess our sin, we agree with God that we are sinners and that we need his help. We should also agree that we have no right to withhold forgiveness from others.

Nevertheless, if we continue to sin without contrition or any effort to live a righteous life, it indicates that our confession of faith in Jesus was never really sincere. "Faith by itself, if it has no works," said James, "is dead" (James 2:17). When you become a Christian, you're not joining a club; you're giving your life to God, who makes specific demands from you as a parent would make of his or her child.

Q: How can I be sure that I will go to heaven?

A: We live by faith, believing God's promises in Scripture are true. Those promises are unwavering in their assurance that our trust in Jesus guarantees our future in heaven. "I write these things to you who believe in the name of the Son of God, so that you may know that you have eternal life," said the apostle John (1 John 5:13). Jesus himself said about his followers, "I give them eternal life, and they will never perish. No one will snatch them out of my hand" (John 10:28).

Sin does not disqualify you because God keeps forgiving you. You cannot accidentally lose your ticket to heaven. In biblical terms, your faith puts

173

you "in Christ," and anyone who is in Christ is a "new creation" (2 Corinthians 5:17). You are transformed. You are part of God's eternal family.

Besides the biblical testimony, we can confirm our standing with God in other ways. One is by examining how God's Spirit living within us transforms our lives. "You will know them by their fruits," Jesus said (Matthew 7:20). What kind of fruit have you been bearing? The Bible describes the fruit of God's Spirit as love, joy, peace, patience, kindness, generosity, faithfulness, gentleness, and self-control (Galatians 5:22–23). Do you see these character traits in your life? If so, that should help convince you that God is working within you. Paul also mentioned a spiritual assurance—"That very Spirit bearing witness with our spirit that we are children of God" (Romans 8:16).

Many Christians go through times of doubting when they worry about their eternal destiny. Don't let those doubts rattle you. Keep going back to the evidence. What does Scripture say? What do the changes in your own life tell you? What sorts of whispers are you hearing from God's Spirit? All of these things should help restore your confidence in God's eternal plans for you.

CHAPTER TEN

ℋow Is the World Going to End?

W e can't help but be amused when we see someone carrying a sign, saying, "The End Is Near!" or something to that effect. These people and their signs seem to appear after every major catastrophe. But do their ludicrous pronouncements mean that an end to the world will never come? The Bible says no. It also tells us why and what signs we should watch for.

Q: Did Jesus predict the end of the world?

A: Jesus spoke explicitly about "the end times" in a sermon that appears both in Matthew 24 and Luke 21. One day as Jesus left the temple complex in Jerusalem, his disciples commented on the beautiful stones that were there. The temple was in the midst of a lengthy rebuilding project, and builders were cutting the stones. Jesus announced that the day would come when all those stones would be toppled. Later, on the Mount of Olives, the disciples asked Jesus when that would occur "and what will be the sign of your coming and of the end of the age?" (Matthew 24:3).

They didn't realize it, but they were asking two different questions—first about the temple and then about his return at the end of this world as we know it. Jesus provided two answers, but it's not entirely clear which answer covers which question. In fact, that ambiguity has given today's Bible scholars a lot to argue about.

Historically, we know that the temple in Jerusalem was destroyed in A.D. 70 about 40 years after Jesus made his statement. The Roman army moved in to quash a Jewish revolt, and they looted and demolished the temple. Jesus had said, "When you see Jerusalem surrounded by armies, then . . . those in Judea must flee to the mountains, and those inside the city must leave it" (Luke 21:20–21). Reportedly many of the Christians in Jerusalem in A.D. 70 did exactly that.

Meanwhile, many other prophecies in this sermon obviously refer to Jesus' second coming and the end of the age. "For as the lightning comes from the east and flashes as far as the west," Jesus said, "so will be the coming of the Son of Man" (Matthew 24:27). Analysts have bickered over Jesus' assurance that "this generation will not pass away until all these things have taken place" (Matthew 24:34). If he was talking about the destruction of the temple in Jerusalem, he was exactly right, for some of his disciples were still alive when that occurred. But others have suggested that Jesus was talking about a future generation that would see the beginning and end of the climactic events of the Second Coming. This verse has led some world watchers to try to calculate a date for Jesus' return. Yet, Jesus said that no one knows the day or the hour of his return, "neither the angels of heaven, nor the Son, but only the Father" (Matthew 24:36). If Jesus didn't have the date circled on his own calendar, we should be careful about claiming that we know the day of his return.

What did Jesus tell us about his return? It will be a surprise, and yet, there will be warning signs to look for. There will be false messiahs, global violence, and natural disasters. The faithful will be persecuted, but the "good news of the kingdom will be proclaimed throughout the world" (Matthew 24:14). In some sense, all these things were true of the period around A.D. 70, as well as at different times up to the present day.

So our confusion continues. Jesus was talking about the first century and times since and events to come, warning that the end might come at any time. "Keep awake therefore, for you do not know on what day your Lord is coming" (Matthew 24:42).

Q: What is the Book of Revelation? Does it give me the secrets of the end times?

A: The last book of the Bible, Revelation, has teased, baffled, and delighted Bible readers for centuries. It is the written record of a vision received by a man named John. Tradition says the apostle John wrote the book while in exile on the island of Patmos. Some scholars today, based on the literary style, think it was another John or a secretary who wrote for the apostle John.

The book starts out as an epistle. John addresses seven churches in Asia Minor (modern Turkey), encouraging and challenging them in their specific situations. But it's not John telling them what they need to hear—it's Jesus. "Listen!" Jesus says to the church at Laodicea. "I am standing at the door, knocking; if you hear my voice and open the door,

I will come in to you and eat with you, and you with me" (Revelation 3:20).

Subsequently, Jesus offers John a guided tour, saying, "Come up here, and I will show you what must take place after this" (Revelation 4:1). A thrill ride is more like it. In highly symbolic language, we glimpse cosmic events. World wars and catastrophes are interspersed with heavenly worship services. We meet beasts and angels carrying trumpets and bowls. The remarkable vision concludes with a "new heaven and a new earth"—and the wedding party of Christ, the Lamb of God.

This style—religious symbolism portraying cosmic events—is known as *apocalyptic;* there were many other apocalypses written in the period about a century before and after Jesus' ministry. Some of these seem to be commentary on current events of the time, while others try to predict the future. The difference with Revelation is that it's Jesus doing the talking, it has a pastoral purpose (to those seven churches), and the early Christians accepted it as an authentic revelation from their Lord. But even they couldn't agree on what it meant.

Four basic methods of interpretation have emerged. The *preterist* view holds that John was speaking symbolically of events in his own time. According to this theory, the Roman Emperor Domitian—who had exiled John, killed many believers, and wanted to be called "Lord and God"—was probably the "Beast." The *historical* view sees the book describing the full sweep of human history. Some scholars even tie the seven churches to particular eras of Christian history—Smyrna the persecuted church of the second and third centuries, Pergamum the heresy-fighting church of the fourth, and so on. The *futurist* view, promoted by many popular books of recent years, sees the events of Revelation unfolding at the "end times," which may be presently at our doorstep. The *poetic* view holds that Revelation presents symbols of ongoing struggles that Christians face but that we shouldn't look for specific events to match up with these descriptions.

Whatever view you take, don't miss the main theme of the book: simply put, *God wins!* There will be bad times for Christians individually and for the church collectively, but our God will emerge victorious, and we will enjoy a glorious future with him.

Q: Will I be able to recognize the "signs" of the end times before it occurs?

A: Jesus clearly indicated that no one knows the exact day of his return, but on several occasions, he talked about the value of watching for "signs." He mentioned cycles in nature and weather patterns that warn us of what's to come. There will be similar signs for his second coming. His message was "Always be ready."

The signs Jesus spoke of were rather generic—war, famine, earthquakes, and persecution of believers. They have occurred quite regularly from his day to ours. Other prophecies, however, especially those in the Books of Daniel and Revelation, hint at specific events that might foretell the end times. The emergence of an independent nation of Israel is one example. This event would have been unthinkable a century ago, but now many Christians see it as a clear sign that the end is near.

Meanwhile, Christians aren't the only ones predicting the end of the world as we know it. In recent years various people have noted such things as global warming, an exploding population, lack of water or food resources, the domination of technology, germ warfare, and nuclear weapons in the hands of terrorists. Some of these dangers might be overstated, but others might be legitimate signs that we're nearing the end.

Some people, however, become so wrapped up in analyzing the signs of Jesus' coming that they forget to get ready for it. We should be sharing the love of God with those around us and not just scaring them to death. We also should be caring for the neediest people in our society, the "least of these," the ones Jesus called his brothers and sisters (Matthew 25:40).

So keep your eyes open for signs of the end. But it does no good to recognize signs if you don't use them as reminders to "be ready." Within his great prophetic sermon of Matthew 24, Jesus told a brief parable about a master who went away, leaving a bond servant in charge of the household. "Blessed is that slave whom his master will find at work when he arrives" (Matthew 24:46). That's the kind of servants we want to be, not sky-gazing and sign-hunting but actively doing the work of the Lord.

Q: What about those popular books that say the "end of the world" will be soon? They scare me. Should I believe them?

A: We must always distinguish between the clear teaching of Scripture and human guesswork, especially in this matter concerning the end times. Many speakers and authors think they have it all figured out, but they really don't. Although they are offering their own interpretation of biblical prophecy, the Bible itself is not that clear on these questions.

For instance, some commentators had insisted that when the European Common Market (ECM) accepted its tenth member, the ECM obviously became the ten-toed Roman Empire prophesied in Daniel 2. Well, at this writing the ECM has more members and counting. Some prophecies mention the "kings of the north" that will threaten Israel, and many authors assumed this meant the Soviet Union. That sounded great during the Cold War; it's a bit less obvious now. In the 1970s, one popular book did the math and predicted that Jesus would return by 1981. (One generation equals 40 years, added to Israel's independence in 1948, equals a 1988 Armageddon date, minus seven years for the tribulation period.) To some, it was a persuasive theory—but it was obviously wrong.

So if you're reading a work of fiction, remember that it's fiction. Predictions most often will not go down exactly that way. If you're reading some analysis of biblical prophecy, remember that it's an opinion, and go back to Scripture to read the original for yourself. What you'll find in Scripture is verification of the idea that Jesus is coming soon. For two thousand years, his return has been "soon." What that means is that this is the next big event on God's agenda. Nothing else needs to happen.

Nevertheless, even in New Testament times, people were asking, "How soon?" Some, it seems, were quitting their jobs to wait for him. To these folks, Paul said, "Anyone unwilling to work should not eat" (2 Thessalonians 3:10). Others were despairing, worrying that Jesus would never return. To these people, Peter said, "With the Lord one day is like a thousand years, and a thousand years are like one day. The Lord is not slow about his promise...the day of the Lord will come like a thief" (2 Peter 3:8–10).

So, yes, the end of the world is coming "soon." Maybe tomorrow. Maybe in the year 3000. In any case, there's no reason to fear. We should welcome his return because he's coming for us, for we will reign with him over a new heaven and a new earth.

Q: If I'm a believer, should I be afraid? What will happen to me?

A: There are different theories about what will happen when Jesus returns. Many are based on Scripture but still interpret key passages differently. One theory holds that, any moment now, a "rapture" will occur in which Jesus will appear in the air and believers will rise up to meet him, going with him to heaven while earth undergoes a seven-year tribulation. Then, after those seven years, Jesus will return *with* the believers to put an end to the Battle of Armageddon and set up his thousand-year reign on earth. This is known as a pre-millennial, pre-tribulation view, meaning that Jesus returns before his thousand-year reign and before the seven-year tribulation. Many modern evangelical books and movies about the end times present this position.

There is also a post-millennial view (in which the church reigns for a thousand years and *then* Jesus returns) and an amillennial view (which doesn't believe in a literal thousand-year reign).

But many Christians hold another pre-millennial view, which is called post-tribulation. In this view, at any moment the seven-year tribulation period will begin, and Christians will suffer for their faith, but after seven years Jesus will return to set up his millennial kingdom with us. (Believe it or not, there's also a "mid-trib" theory, in which we go through some tribulation, but the rapture occurs before things become really bad.)

Confused yet? The basic difference between pre-trib and post-trib is the answer to the question, *Will Christians go through the tribulation?* Pre-tribs go to 1 Thessalonians 4:13–17 to support the rapture idea. Post-tribs say that 2 Thessalonians 2:3–4 corrects that notion. You can study the pertinent Scriptures for yourself.

If you're getting spooked by the end-times novels you're reading, relax. Most of these are written from a pre-trib view, which means that those characters going through the tribulation have become believers *after* the rapture. If you're a Christian now (in this view), you'll get raptured out before things get bad, so you have nothing to worry about. But if the post-tribs are right, and you *do* have to go through these seven years of trouble, you might legitimately be concerned about how you'll fare.

Nonetheless, Jesus made this good-news, bad-news promise to his followers: "In the world you face persecution. But take courage; I have conquered the world!" (John 16:33). Tribulation is already an everyday occurrence in many nations of the world. In various periods of history, many believers have suffered for their faith. Yet, Jesus saw no reason for his followers to be afraid, even in those times of trouble. He is ultimately in charge, and he will provide the strength needed to get through persecution.

"Do not fear, for I am with you," said the Lord through Isaiah. "Do not be afraid, for I am your God; I will strengthen you, I will help you, I will uphold you with my victorious right hand" (Isaiah 41:10). Those assurances apply to us as well, whether we face teasing, discrimination, violence, or seven years of increasing tribulation.

Q: What will happen on the "Day of Judgment"?

A: The Old Testament prophets often warned of the "Day of the Lord" in which God would judge the people of all nations, including Israel. In fact, the earth itself would tremble on this awe-filled occasion. The New Testament picked up the theme of Judgment Day, but here it was sometimes called the "Day of Christ." In fact, Jesus described this event by telling several stories about masters who went away for a while and then returned to evaluate what their servants had done in the meantime. So the idea is a strong one throughout Scripture: God will judge the people of earth, punishing the wicked and rewarding the good.

But it's not that clear-cut, as the apostle Paul strongly noted in several letters. No one is good enough to meet God's perfect standards. We all deserve God's condemnation, except for the fact that Jesus took the punishment for us. As a result, "There is therefore now no condemnation for those who are in Christ Jesus" (Romans 8:1).

So we can only imagine that the fearsome judgment of God goes something like this: We stand before

God with all our faults; the Almighty Father is ready to judge our sin; but Jesus says, "Wait! This is one of mine. I paid for the sins." God is just, but he is also faithful. He must punish sinners, but Jesus took that punishment on the cross, which results in God being faithful to his promise to count our faith in Jesus as righteousness.

There are some indications in the New Testament that Christians will answer to Christ for our deeds (1 Corinthians 3:12–15). This is not a matter of heaven or hell but of rewards, or "crowns," we might receive as appreciation for work well done (2 Timothy 4:8). Thus, the Book of Revelation seems to speak of two judgments, one before the millennium, which might be this crown-awarding event for believers (Revelation 20:4–6), and then a "Great White Throne" judgment where God finally judges sin and condemns the wicked to eternal punishment (Revelation 20:11–14).

Q: Will God destroy the world or renew it? Why does the Bible refer to a "new heaven and earth"?

A: Both Testaments speak of the elements of earth "melting" on the judgment day of the Lord. This might be a poetic way to describe the magnitude of that moment or it might literally happen that way. On the "day of God," according to 2 Peter, "the heavens will be set ablaze and dissolved, and the elements will melt with fire[.] But, in accordance with his promise, we wait for new heavens and a new earth, where righteousness is at home" (2 Peter 3:12–13). It only makes sense that the dissolving and melting of earth would create the need for a new one. (By the way, "the heavens" in this case means merely the sky and not God's actual kingdom.)

One of the recurring characteristics of the Bible is the interaction of the physical and spiritual. Whereas some other religions focus on spiritual ideas and practically ignore anything physical, Christianity (rooted in Judaism) fuses body and soul together. Our physical responses to God are as important as our spiritual responses. In the coming resurrection, it's not just the soul that lives on, but we will receive new bodies as well. And the physical world itself

joins with humanity in praising God, suffering
the effects of sin, longing for God's redemption,
receiving God's judgment, and becoming a "new
creation."

Of course, we don't know the mechanics of this
re-creation of heaven and earth. Will God start from
scratch again? Or will he just sandblast the earth,
spackle it, and put on a new coat of paint? It could
be a "new earth" in the same way that you'd
remodel and get a "new kitchen." But the key point
is that God is re-creating, starting over in a brand-
new relationship with both humanity and the
physical world.

Q: Will there be a resurrection of those people
who have already died? If so, and if they
are already in heaven, how will that work?

A: Yes, there will be a resurrection of the dead.
When the New Testament says we are risen with
Christ, it's not just talking about a spiritual body.
There will be a physical resurrection associated with
Christ's return and the final judgment. "The dead in
Christ will rise first," said Paul, describing the Second

Coming. Moreover, those who are still alive will
"meet the Lord in the air" (1 Thessalonians 4:16–17).
"For the trumpet will sound," he said elsewhere,
"and the dead will be raised imperishable"
(1 Corinthians 15:52).

Of course, this raises all sorts of logistical issues.
What of decay? Is there anything left of bodies that
died a thousand years ago? Maybe not, but we have
a God who created human bodies from the dust of
the earth to begin with. Certainly he can form us
new, imperishable bodies from available materials.
The Bible depicts a reclaiming of bodies from their
final resting places. "And the sea gave up the dead
that were in it, Death and Hades gave up the dead
that were in them" (Revelation 20:13). Perhaps the
souls will re-inhabit these regenerated bodies in
mid-air. We can trust God to work out the details,
and we can also be assured that our new immortal
bodies will be beautiful to behold.